Missionaries

The Christian
Social Club Adventure

Reverend John Paul Emmanuel

Valentine Publishing House
Denver, Colorado

For more information about special discounts or bulk purchases, please contact Valentine Publishing House at 1-877-266-5289.

Publisher's Cataloging-in-Publication Data
    Missionaries / Reverend John Paul Emmanuel.
    Volume One / The Christian Social Club Adventure.

    p. cm.
    LCCN: 2023951969
    ISBN-10: 0-9994908-1-8
    ISBN-13: 978-0-9994908-1-5

    1. Christian Fiction.
    2. Spiritual Warfare.
    3. Evangelization.

    PS3562.A315R44 2024
    813'.54–dc22
    2023951969

Printed in the United States of America.

*"All authority in heaven and on earth has
been given to me. Go therefore and make disciples
of all nations, baptizing them in the name of
the Father and of the Son and of the Holy Spirit,
and teaching them to obey everything that
I have commanded you. And remember,
I am with you always, to the end of the age."*

Matthew 28:18–20

1ˢᵗ CHAPTER

When Overwatch summoned the warriors, twelve angelic beings descended upon the property with their swords drawn ready for battle. When the leader of the demonic principality, named Phantalon, realized something was wrong, he ascended through the roof of the building and said to the intruders, "This is our domain. What are you doing here?"

All the angels remained silent except for the commander, who said, "You are not allowed to interfere with the missionaries or we will execute judgment upon you immediately."

"Send out the bouncer," Phantalon cried out as he hovered over the parking lot.

As the demons prepared to defend their territory, Michelle turned down a side street and parked her white, four-door Jeep on a hillside overlooking the parking lot. From this vantage point, the missionaries were able to count fifty-two cars, not including a white limousine that was parked in front of the main entrance.

"Let's pray for protection," Michelle said.

"I don't want to do anything illegal," Daniel said as he put on his jacket.

"It's not illegal," Matthew said. "If it will make you feel better, we can pray the prayer of authority that was given to Joshua, only with more power by invoking the name of Jesus. This is our city, it belongs to God, and as his servants, we have an obligation to take authority over every place where our feet tread. We have a responsibility to drive these evil perverts out of our sphere of influence."

After removing a Bible from the center compartment of her Jeep, Michelle opened it to the Book of Joshua and said, "'Be strong and courageous; do not be frightened or dismayed, for the Lord your God is with you wherever you go. Every place that the sole of your foot will tread upon I have given to you, as I promised to Moses.'"[1]

"Let's assume the authority that God has given us and drive these evil perverts out of our community," Matthew said. "We are going to take authority over every place where the soles of our feet tread and ask God to send an assignment of warring angels to strike down and destroy everything evil or demonic in, on or around this property."

"Let's also pray for the women who work there," Michelle said, "that God minister to the wounded parts of their hearts so that they can break free from this lifestyle."

"Here comes another limo," Daniel said.

As the neon red-and-white lights that displayed the words "Gentlemen's Club" continued to flash in the distance, Matthew took three plastic water bottles from his backpack and handed one to Michelle.

"What's this for?" Daniel asked as he received the other container.

"It's holy water," Matthew said. "Just loosen the cap and allow a trail of water to drip out on the ground as we take authority over the property. The water will evaporate, but the blessed salt will remain. Tiny particles of salt will penetrate the concrete and it will remain on the parking lot for a very long time. By laying down blessed salt, combined with the power of God, our deliverance prayers have the ability to drive these evil perverts out of our community."

As the missionaries approached the strip club, they unscrewed the caps on their water bottles and allowed the holy water to drip out on the ground while they exorcised the property. The first pass consisted of a wider perimeter around the cars and the sidewalk in front of the main entrance. As they walked along, Matthew started splashing the parked cars with holy water as he prayed for the men who frequented the club.

After making several passes around the parking lot, the missionaries drew closer to the main entrance. Daniel used the remaining water in his bottle to splash the exterior of the building. As he drew closer, he could hear the sound of rock and roll music vibrating through the walls. When the missionaries walked behind the building on the third pass, the club's bouncer opened the back door and said, "What are you doing here? This is private property."

For a brief second, the missionaries froze with fear. Daniel wanted to run, and Matthew wanted to fight, but Michelle said, "I wanted to inquire about a job. These are my friends, Matthew and Daniel."

"You need to come back during the day to speak with the club's manager," the man said.

"Will you please tell me the manager's name?" Michelle asked.

"The owner's name is Charlie," the bouncer said. "He usually arrives around eleven o'clock in the morning."

After the missionaries thanked the bouncer for his assistance, they turned around and walked away as quickly as possible.

"Let's keep walking in case we're being followed," Matthew said as they passed the street where Michelle's Jeep was parked.

"Did you see how big that guy was?" Daniel said.

"You're looking for a job interview," Matthew said. "What were you thinking?"

"I couldn't think of anything else," Michelle said.

"I thought it was brilliant," Daniel said. "Now that we know the owner's name, we can pray for his conversion on a daily basis."

"Let's keep walking around the block before going

back to the Jeep," Matthew said. "I want to make sure we're not being followed."

After the missionaries left the property, Phantalon said to the demonic spirits under his control, "Follow those despicable monkeys. I want to know every detail of their filthy lives."

"If you interfere with the missionaries, we will execute judgment upon you immediately," the angelic commander said.

"We have the right to tempt those carnal animals anytime we want," Phantalon said. "Once they make agreements with us through their sins, we have the right to enter into their lives and give them everything they deserve."

"Your time is short," the commander said as the angelic warriors departed.

"Once we identify the big baboon's weaknesses, I'm sure we can fulfill his heart's desires," Phantalon said, following the angelic warriors into the night sky.

After returning to her Jeep, Michelle said, "I think we should go back during the day. I could feel the Lord's love and concern for the women who work there."

"I was praying against the club's finances," Daniel said. "I asked El Shaddai to put the club's owner out of business, to hinder his cash flow and turn away his patrons. I also asked Adonai to force the strippers to leave our community."

"How much money do you think an exotic dancer

gets paid per night?" Michelle asked.

"It probably depends on the services that she provides," Daniel said.

* * *

After driving back to Holy Trinity Catholic Parish, the missionaries walked down a set of concrete stairs that led into the church basement.

"I will make some chai tea," Michelle said as Matthew turned on the fluorescent lights that started flickering for several seconds before illuminating the cafeteria.

When Daniel took a seat at one of the tables that was located in the center of the basement between the kitchen and stage, he said, "What an adventure."

"I think we need to go back for another round next weekend," Matthew said.

"What about our Valentine's Day dance?" Michelle asked.

"You're right," Matthew said. "Let's go back the weekend after next."

As the missionaries continued discussing the excitement they experienced that evening, Father O'Connor walked down the set of stairs that led into the church basement.

"I saw the lights on and wanted to investigate," the middle-aged priest said who was wearing a black, short-sleeved shirt with a white collar.

"It's just us," Michelle said. "Would you like to join us for tea? We are working through the last-minute details for our Valentine's Day dance."

"No tea for me," Father said. "I have to attend a rosary vigil at the chancery tonight in honor of the Blessed Mother's intentions."

"How do you know what those intentions are?" Michelle asked.

"That's part of the sacred mysteries of prayer," Father O'Connor said. "We ask God to grant every desire of the Blessed Mother's heart. That's because we're all one big family. By the way, did you know Saint Valentine was arrested for marrying young couples in secret, and he was martyred for his faith on February fourteenth?"

"I didn't know that," Michelle said as she served the chai tea. "Are you sure you wouldn't like some?"

"I have to be going," Father said as he turned to leave.

"Is that true about Saint Valentine being arrested for marrying young couples in secret?" Michelle asked.

"Let me search the Internet," Daniel said, opening his laptop computer. "According to one source, the Roman emperor passed a law making Christian marriage illegal during the third century. The theory was that Rome needed young men to join the army and fight in wars. If a young man was married, he was expected to stay at home to care for his wife and children.

"Even though the Roman emperor passed the law, Saint Valentine not only converted a lot of young people to Christianity, but he also married them in secret. When he was arrested, he proclaimed the Gospel message to the prison guards, and he also prayed for an official's daughter who was blind.

"Before Saint Valentine was executed for marrying young couples in secret, he wrote the official's daughter a love letter from God, and signed the letter 'your Valentine.' Hence the tradition of sending love letters on February fourteenth."

"That's very interesting," Michelle said, "although I still think we need to find another location for our Jclub events."

"I agree," Daniel said. "Conducting events in the church basement may be harming our sales. We need a place that's more modern and happening."

"I like working here because Father has been giving us free rent all this time," Matthew said.

"Maybe after five years in the basement, it's time for a change of venue," Michelle said. "Besides, Father makes me uncomfortable with all his rosary vigils."

"We already have the address for the dance printed on the advertising flyers," Matthew said. "It's too late to change locations this year, but if we can find a free dance hall next year, I would be in favor of a different venue."

After the missionaries worked out the remaining details regarding the Valentine's Day dance, Michelle turned to Matthew and said, "Although it's girl's night out, it would be great if you could join us Saturday evening. You would be surrounded by beautiful women all night long."

"I appreciate the invitation," Matthew said, "but I was looking forward to preparing a nice dinner at home, watching a movie and enjoying some quiet time."

"Are you sure?" Michelle said. "You could be my escort to the hottest *faire la fête* in town."

"Let me think about it," Matthew said.

"Call me if you change your mind," Michelle said.

After Michelle left for the evening, an assignment of demonic spirits that Phantalon sent entered the church basement to gather intelligence on the missionaries. Because they were invisible and completely silent, they could hover directly under the flickering fluorescent lights without being detected. The silent intruders wanted to discover their enemy's weaknesses so they could coordinate a deadly attack.

"Why don't you want to date her?" Daniel asked. "She's gorgeous, and she obviously likes you."

"I don't want to mess up our working relationship," Matthew said. "She's the best event coordinator we could ever find. Without her help, we wouldn't have any activities, and if we did, they would all be lame."

"That's all the more reason to get serious with her," Daniel said. "You have such a beautiful working relationship. You get along so well together, complementing each other as the perfect couple."

"I like Michelle a lot," Matthew said. "She's talented, intelligent and always surrounded by a thousand friends, but intimate relationships are messy and extremely painful when they don't work out, especially when you don't have the Lord's permission to date or get intimately involved with another person."

"Have you ever asked the Lord's permission to date Michelle?" Daniel asked.

"If you want to know the truth, deep in my heart, I'm still hurt over my ex-fiancée," Matthew said. "Although we seemed like the perfect match, it was a disaster. We fought all the time, and we were both miserable."

"It doesn't seem fair to compare Michelle to your college girlfriend," Daniel said. "I'm sure you know the Bible passage about being unequally yoked.[2] What partnership does light have with darkness? Or what fellowship does a Spirit-filled Christian have with a worldly woman from your past?"

"All my core principles come from Scripture," Matthew said as he picked up a Bible that was lying on the shelf in the storage room. "In the First Letter to the Corinthians, Saint Paul wanted Christians with a serious calling on their lives to remain single, as he was single. Then in chapter seven, Saint Paul says, 'To the unmarried and the widows I say that it is well for them to remain unmarried as I am.'"[3]

"What about the sacred institution of marriage?" Daniel said. "In the Book of Genesis, Yahweh said that it was not good for a man to be alone, so he created woman as a partner."[4]

"That's from the Old Testament," Matthew said. "In the New Covenant, Saint Paul says, 'Are you bound to a wife? Do not seek to be free. Are you free from a wife? Do not seek a wife. But if you marry, you do not sin, and if a virgin marries, she does not sin. Yet those who marry will experience distress in this life.'[5]

"Then in the following verse, Saint Paul says, 'I want you to be free from anxieties. The unmarried man is anxious about the affairs of the Lord, how to please the Lord; but the married man is anxious about the affairs of the world, how to please his wife, and his interests are divided.'[6] The same is true for women. Once a man or a woman enters into marriage, those people are no longer free to serve the Lord with their full devotion, and their interests become divided."

"How can the president of Jclub have such a negative outlook on marriage?" Daniel asked.

"It's not negative," Matthew said. "A better description of my attitude toward marriage would be Biblically based. Because Sacred Scripture says that a man's interests will be divided, and that he will experience distress in this life, I'm thinking you had better have the Lord's permission before dating a woman. Besides, marriage is only temporary, and there's no marriage in heaven."[7]

"My parents have been blessed with many years of a fruitful and prosperous marriage," Daniel said. "Every time they fight over something small, it's usually an indicator of a deeper issue. After they invited Yeshua into their lives and hearts, they have always grown in holiness. After watching my parent's transformation process for many years, I believe that Yeshua allows conflicts in Christian marriages to help couples grow together in holiness, so that they may deepen their love for each other."

"I know your parents have a great relationship," Matthew said. "If you're called to get married and you have God's permission to date and get married, then I'm sure God will bless your union—but what happens if you're not called to get married?

"What happens if I'm called to be single like Saint Paul? Called to be an evangelist who travels the world proclaiming the Gospel message? Called to move with the same power as the Apostle who was shipwrecked for a night and a day, beaten with rods, stoned to the point of death, in toil and hardships, through many sleepless nights, and yet he still kept going?"[8]

"That would be a powerful calling," Daniel said.

"If I'm called to be like the Apostle Paul, I had better fulfill my calling in Christ. If I'm called to be married and raise a family, then I had better fulfill my calling in Christ. Either way, I'm required to be an obedient servant of God, to seek the will of my Master and accomplish his will in my life.

"If I'm not called to date Michelle, then it doesn't matter how attractive she is; if I enter into a sinful relationship with her outside of God's will, it will only end in disaster. I have already learned that lesson the hard way with my fiancée from college, and I'm not going to make the same mistake twice."

"That's what I admire about you," Daniel said. "You are constantly seeking Yeshua's will for your life. I only wish I had your integrity when it comes to women."

"Come on, it's getting late," Matthew said. "I have to get back home."

* * *

After the missionaries went their separate ways, the demonic spirits returned to Phantalon and said, "The little monkey with dark fur is the weakest link. He has insecurity issues. He wants to be wealthy and successful, yet he's working at a Christian singles club."

"We can take him down with sexual sins," another demon said. "All we need to do is send in the perfect honeypot and wait for him to take the bait."

"What about the big baboon?" Phantalon asked.

"Another principality has been attacking him since college with very little success," another demonic spirit said. "He's advanced in spiritual warfare, but if we conduct an assault on his emotional wounds, making him angry at everything, we can drive him deeper into isolation."

"We can also break apart their social club with law enforcement by sending in one of our creepophiles," another demonic spirit said.

"I also want to exterminate the female chimpanzee," Phantalon said as he dispatched the demonic spirits to carry out their assignments.

2nd CHAPTER

Several hours before the Valentine's Day dance was scheduled to begin, Michelle and her friends arrived early to decorate the church basement. One of Michelle's friends, named Tiffany, rented a helium tank so that the girls could inflate over three hundred red, white and pink balloons.

As the band members were setting up their musical instruments, and Jason was performing the necessary lighting and sound tests, Michelle was struggling in the kitchen trying to remove an obstruction from the ice machine. When Matthew arrived, he said, "Let me help you with that."

"I have more soft drinks and sparkling water in my Jeep," Michelle said, "if you would be so kind as to bring them inside."

The first youth pastor to arrive was Scott Samson from Green Valley Presbyterian Church. He brought his entire youth group of twenty-seven members on a school bus that he borrowed from Jefferson High

School. Other youth pastors arrived in minivans loaded with teens, while the older members of Jclub filled the parking lot with their own vehicles.

"I think it's time to begin," Michelle said. After walking up the steps to the stage, she removed the microphone from the stand and said, "Welcome to Jclub's annual Valentine's Day dance! I'm so happy you are here. We usually start the dance by forming a giant conga line; and then Jason has some new dance combinations that he wants to share with us, including the Macarena, Electric Slide and Cupid's Shuffle."

After Michelle handed the microphone to Jason, she gathered her closest friends together to form a conga line. As she danced around the room, she reached out for the hands of any shy teenagers who were seated around the perimeter and gracefully incorporated them into the line. After the first Jamaican-sounding song with a progressive beat ended, Jason was able to transition the entire dance floor into the Boot Scootin' Boogie.

At the end of the evening, many of the youth pastors approached Matthew and Michelle to thank them for providing an excellent event. "It was such a blessing for my group," a youth pastor named Douglas said. "It felt like you raised everybody's confidence levels. I could see the joy of the Lord in my members' eyes after you made them feel like a valuable part of the community."

"That's because they are valuable," Michelle said. "Please take some flyers for our coffee shop meet and greet this Wednesday. It would be good to see you there so we can catch up on everything."

After the band members finished loading the musical instruments and sound equipment into their van and departed for the evening, Matthew approached Daniel and asked, "How did we do?"

"We sold two hundred and sixty full-price tickets and seventeen discounted tickets," Daniel said. "We also received a three hundred dollar donation from Mrs. Donohue and a few other smaller donations from parents who thanked us for helping their kids."

"What's wrong?" Matthew asked as Michelle approached the table to join the conversation.

"Did you see that older man who was stalking the younger kids all night?" Michelle asked. "He had two girls cornered behind the stage before I came over to rescue them."

"Everyone who entered had a membership card," Daniel said.

"Where did he get a membership card?" Michelle asked.

"His name is Chester," Matthew said. "I thought he looked a little too old when he stopped by last week, but he paid in cash and gave us a hundred-dollar donation. He made it sound like he was interested in helping the kids and wanted to volunteer some time."

"That guy was giving me a creepy feeling all night," Michelle said. "I thought we had an age limit for members. That guy is way older than twenty-eight. He's probably closer to forty."

"I didn't check his age," Matthew said. "He just moved here from Cincinnati, and he didn't have a physical address, but because he gave us a donation, I didn't think it was a problem. If you want, I will follow up with him to get more information."

"I think we need a background check on that guy," Michelle said.

"Let's pray for protection and thank God for a successful evening," Matthew said. "You did an excellent job setting everything up, and everybody was very happy. Besides, it's getting late. Let me walk you to your Jeep, and we can finish cleaning up tomorrow."

* * *

The next Jclub event was scheduled for Wednesday at the Château Coffee Company, located in a trendy part of the downtown area that was surrounded by luxurious lofts and upscale shops. The interior design consisted of a reddish-gray brick facade, and the owners specialized in serving the finest European lattes and cappuccinos. Soft leather sofas and reclining chairs, arranged in tight patterns in the main serving area, provided the guests with a casual yet relaxing atmosphere.

The Château was also one of Michelle's favorite places to meet with her friends and socialize, but around seven o'clock that evening, Chester arrived and began hitting on Barbara, a petite girl with sandy brown hair. Before long, Chester started telling dirty jokes to several of Barbara's friends.

When Chester approached two young women, Kimberly and Karen, he asked them about their sex lives. Because the girls were appalled by his questions, Kimberly responded by saying, "This is Jclub! The letter J stands for Jesus. We're all Christians, and Christians don't have sex outside of a God-approved marriage. It's a very serious sin called *fornication*. Maybe you should read about it in your Bible and leave us alone."

After all the Jclub members left for the evening, Michelle tried calling Matthew, but his phone was turned off. When she walked outside and halfway down the block, she recognized Chester sitting in the driver's seat of an older green Ford van with a plumbing logo on the side. She pretended not to notice him and kept walking, looking in the opposite direction as she passed by.

When she arrived at her Jeep, the green van started to pull away from the curb, so she quickly jumped into her vehicle, started the engine and began following him to see where he was going. The green van turned down Market Street and made a right turn on Broadway.

Michelle was careful to keep her distance, allowing several other vehicles to get between her and the van so when Chester looked in his rearview mirror he wouldn't realize that he was being followed.

After making a right turn on Downing Street, the green van entered an on-ramp for the interstate highway and drove twelve miles to Paradise Valley. Because there was very little traffic at that time of night, it became difficult for Michelle to follow too closely. She needed to allow several blocks of distance between them; and at one point, she lost sight of Chester, but after circling back around the block, she discovered the green Ford van with the plumbing logo parked in the driveway on Maplewood Drive.

After passing the house, she pulled over to call Matthew, but his phone was still turned off. When she was praying for guidance, two young boys walked by her Jeep. They appeared to be around twelve years old and were heading in the direction of Chester's house. After they passed by, Michelle sank a little lower in the front seat and adjusted her rearview mirror to see what would happen next.

The boys stopped in front of Chester's house, and after looking around to see if anyone was watching, they walked up the steps and knocked on the door. When Chester opened the door, he hugged the boys and invited them inside.

Because Chester lived in a crime-ridden part of the city, Michelle started her Jeep and drove to Holy Trinity Catholic Parish to see if Matthew was working late. Because all the lights in the basement had been turned off, she drove to his apartment and knocked on the door. When he answered, she said, "I have been calling you all evening and your phone was off."

"I'm sorry," Matthew said. "I just wanted to chill tonight. Did you have a good turnout at the meet and greet?"

"Everything was fine until Chester showed up and started harassing our guests," Michelle said. "He was parked outside in a green plumbing van, so I followed him home."

"You followed him home?" Matthew asked in a surprised tone of voice.

"He lives in Paradise Valley, and there were two young boys who knocked on his door. They appeared to know Chester and went inside his house. He's probably selling drugs, or giving away free drugs so that he can gain their trust, and who knows what else he does with those kids once he gains access to their lives."

"What do you want me to do about it?" Matthew asked.

"You should see his house," Michelle said. "The siding was practically falling off and several windows were covered with plywood. There was a vacant lot next door that was littered with trash and old tires. It looked like a scene out of a horror movie, with gangs of delinquents prowling the streets late at night looking for trouble."

"I'm so glad you're okay," Matthew said. "Please come in so we can pray together."

After Michelle took a seat at the kitchen table, she said, "I think we need to call the police."

"He hasn't committed any crimes that we know about," Matthew said.

"He was telling dirty jokes and harassing my friends with his sexually perverted innuendos," Michelle said.

"I think we should inform Chester about a change in our membership policy," Matthew said. "If he is older than twenty-eight, I will tell him we need to cancel his membership and refund his money."

"What about the boys who went inside his house?" Michelle asked.

"Let's pray and ask God for guidance," Matthew said. "Maybe Daniel will have some ideas, or we can ask Father O'Connor if the Diocese has any resources from the Safe Environment Program that we can utilize."

"If Chester shows up at another event, we could

record him on our cell phones propositioning minors for sex," Michelle said.

"Let's pray for guidance," Matthew said. "The last thing we need to do is create enemies who will follow us around in an attempt to sabotage our events."

After Matthew and Michelle spent some time in prayer that evening, they agreed to meet at the church the next morning to discuss the situation with Father O'Connor.

* * *

When Daniel arrived for the meeting, he said, "I have some good news! There were a lot fewer cars in the strip club's parking lot this week."

"I still want to go back for another prayer walk," Matthew said.

"I have been praying for God to make the property invisible," Daniel said. "That way when people drive by, all they see is a vacant lot, similar to an abandoned house that people drive by every day and never even notice that it's there."

"That's an interesting prayer strategy," Michelle said. "What do you think we should do about Chester?"

"The Department of Justice maintains a national database of registered sex offenders," Daniel said. "If you tell me his address, I will check the registry for his name."

"How do you know these things?" Michelle asked.

"I learned about it on a television show," Daniel said as he opened his laptop to search the database.

"Sure enough, Chester is a registered sex offender."

As Daniel was still speaking, Father O'Connor walked down the stairs and into the church basement.

"I'm so happy you were able to meet with us this morning," Matthew said.

"What seems to be the problem?" Father asked.

"There's an older man who has attended several of our events, and we just found out that he's a registered sex offender," Michelle said.

"I knew a young man many years ago who wanted to become a priest," Father O'Connor said. "When he was in high school, his girlfriend accused him of inappropriately touching her. After the girl's parents got involved, they persuaded the police to arrest him for rape. Although the young man accepted a plea deal for a lesser charge, the court system branded him as a sex offender, and now he has to register with a database for the rest of his life. To make matters worse, with all the recent sex scandals within the Church, our Bishop wouldn't allow him to become a priest."

"After discussing the situation with Michelle last night, I wanted to revoke Chester's membership and refund his money," Matthew said. "Is there anything else we should do?"

"Why do you want to persecute this man any further?" Father O'Connor asked.

"We wanted to report the situation to you because the Diocese may have additional resources available from the Safe Environment Program," Matthew said.

"I think we should pray the rosary for twelve consecutive days to Our Lady of Mount Carmel for this man's conversion," Father O'Connor said. "I will also offer up my daily devotions for the next two weeks for this man's intentions."

"We were thinking of contacting the police," Michelle said. "It seems like he joined Jclub to gain access to our younger members."

"Please don't create a media scandal for the Diocese," Father said as he turned to leave the basement. "I'm sure Our Lady of Mount Carmel will provide all the blessings that you desire."

After Father left the church basement, Michelle said, "What does that mean? He wants us to pray to Our Lady of Mount Carmel for Chester's intentions! What if Chester's only intention is to molest little children? Is Our Lady of Mount Carmel going to help Chester accomplish his perverted agenda?"

"After you left my apartment last night, I felt our first priority should be to protect our members," Matthew said. "We can do this by revoking Chester's membership and refunding his money. We can also alert our members to be on the lookout for Chester. Now that we know he's a registered sex offender, we can make an anonymous complaint to the Paradise Valley Police Department and ask them to watch his house for young children who have been frequenting the property, but I want to leave Jclub out of the police report."

"That sounds like a wise plan," Daniel said. "We

should be very careful when dealing with the police, especially when we can't prove that a crime existed. Besides, the Jewish people have had many unpleasant encounters with the police and other government enforcement agencies throughout the centuries, many of which have been perpetrated by evil. Don't forget that the police are spiritual vessels as well. They can be filled with the Holy Spirit to serve and protect our community or with demonic spirits who only want to arrest people and lock them up in concentration camps."

"I never knew you didn't like the police," Michelle said.

"I will deal with Chester tomorrow," Matthew said. "I will also attend the Metropolitan Art Gallery event on Friday night to make sure he doesn't show up again."

"What if Chester does show up?" Michelle asked.

"Then we'll take him out back and teach him some manners," Matthew said.

"That's when the police will really get involved," Daniel said.

"Don't worry, Chester is not going to attend any more Jclub events," Matthew said. "I will deal with him tomorrow."

"Thank you for protecting our members," Michelle said, standing up to leave.

* * *

When Phantalon summoned the demonic spirits that had been assigned to attack the missionaries, he said, "Give me a progress report."

"We have already introduced our honeypot into their social events," one of the demonic spirits said. "We are working with our assets in the area to cause the maximum amount of damage to their operations. We have also finished acquiring intelligence on the female chimpanzee."

"What's your plan of attack?" Phantalon asked.

"When another principality eliminated her father and younger sister many years ago, it formed a deep emotional wound that we can access," another demon said. "By manipulating her emotional insecurities, we can make her act compulsively, and then we can prompt her to make bad decisions."

"That's all you have?" Phantalon asked. "Find a way to eliminate them quickly!"

"They are all very serious Christians," another demon said. "They are constantly praying for protection, and they have an assignment of angelic warriors standing guard over them day and night."

"Find a way to make them sin so that we can gain access to their lives," Phantalon demanded.

3rd CHAPTER

The Metropolitan Art Gallery was located in a popular part of the downtown district in a two-story building. The main floor consisted of a small cafe in the back of the gallery that was surrounded by round, silver tables. All the walls were painted with a glossy white finish, and located in the center of the display area, three triangular columns were used to present the modern artist's paintings.

The second floor consisted of wide-open spaces with metal bench seats that had been thoughtfully placed throughout the display area so that patrons could sit down and discuss the artist's latest creations. Lighting for the gallery was provided by tiny spotlights mounted on long electrical tracts that were attached to black rafters in the open ceiling.

When Michelle arrived, she immediately greeted the gallery owner by saying, "Monica, it's so good to see you. I can't wait to experience your latest collection."

Over the next several hours, eighty-five Jclub

members arrived and spent time socializing with the other guests. Michelle set up a table on the second floor with cheese and crackers, sparkling water and cranberry juice, while the cafe on the main floor served a variety of croissant sandwiches, cappuccinos and lattes.

When Matthew arrived, he greeted Daniel, who was giving an attractive young lady a tour of the gallery.

"Have you seen Michelle?" Matthew asked.

"She's serving drinks on the second level," Daniel said. "I'm sure you remember Aurora."

"How could I forget Aurora?" Matthew said as he reached out to shake her hand. "I'm so happy you were able to attend this evening. I trust Daniel will introduce you to all the other members and make sure you feel welcome."

"Thank you for your hospitality," Aurora said. "Daniel has been providing me with a very informative tour of the gallery."

"Let me check on Michelle, and I will come back to visit later," Matthew said as he headed toward a metal staircase. When he reached the top landing, Michelle was speaking with an older gentleman who was wearing a yellow T-shirt with a large green marijuana leaf. He was accompanied by a tall, slender, younger woman with blonde hair who was wearing a florescent pink jumpsuit with matching sunglasses. Because Matthew didn't want to interrupt their conversation, he decided to wait near a display of porcelain vases.

After Michelle gracefully ended the conversation

with the couple, Matthew approached her and asked, "Did Chester show up tonight?"

"He's been prowling around, interfering with our guests all evening," Michelle said. "What happened? I thought you were going to refund his membership fee."

"I met with Chester and refunded his money," Matthew said. "I was very professional and explained our age policy, but we can't stop him from attending this event because the art gallery is open to the public."

"We could ask Monica to escort him off her property," Michelle said.

"That would create a big scene and put Monica in a very uncomfortable situation," Matthew said. "I think this is an attack from the enemy, and we should ignore Chester this evening. I think the devil sent him into Jclub to cause problems, and we don't want to fall into the devil's trap."

"What do you think we should do?" Michelle asked.

"Let's ignore him tonight and pretend he's not even here," Matthew said. "Tomorrow, we can visit the police station in Paradise Valley and file a report that explains how minors have been visiting a convicted sex offender's home late at night. After we file a police report, we can warn our members to stay away from him."

"What if we started taking pictures of Chester every time he visits one of our events?" Michelle asked.

"Through the power of prayer, we will drive the devil and his perverted puppets out of our lives," Matthew said. "Why don't you continue interacting with our guests while I keep an eye on Chester and start prayer-walking the perimeter of the room."

"I have to leave early tonight," Michelle said, "but I will meet you at the church tomorrow morning."

* * *

The next day, Michelle was waiting in the church basement when Daniel arrived. She had prepared a ripe papaya with slices of lime for a mid-morning snack, along with a steaming pot of ginseng tea. A few minutes later, Matthew arrived and said to Daniel, "Tell us about your time with Aurora. It looked like you spent the entire evening together."

"She gave me her phone number and wanted to go out for dinner Saturday night," Daniel said with an enthusiastic glow on his face.

"Congratulations!" Matthew said. "I haven't seen you this happy in a long time."

"Would you like some fresh fruit?" Michelle asked.

"What's the matter?" Matthew asked. "Please don't tell me that you don't like Aurora."

"I'm very happy that Daniel is happy," Michelle said. "It's just that I have spent some time with Aurora in our women's fellowship group right after she signed up."

"Please continue," Daniel said. "I would like to hear what you have to say."

"There was this thing that Aurora was doing with her Bible that was very disturbing," Michelle said. "It felt more New Age than Christian."

"Go on," Matthew said.

"As you know, the Bible is the Word of God," Michelle said. "As Christians, we can read God's Word and allow God to speak to us through his Word. We can also meditate on God's Word and ask God questions about his Word. The problem is that Aurora was using her Bible as an object of divination almost like a fortune teller would use the lines on a person's hand to deliver a spiritual message from God."

"Can you give us an example?" Daniel asked.

"Let me see your palm," Michelle said.

When Daniel extended his hand, Michelle ran her index finger across his palm in a diagonal direction and said, "Do you see this line? It means you are going to be very rich and successful one day. Now give me a Bible and allow me to open God's Word to a random page, and I will give you the same prophecy."

As Michelle opened her Bible to the Book of Psalms, she ran her finger down the page and said, "According to this verse, you are going to be very rich and successful one day.

"So what's the difference between giving you a psychic reading from a daily horoscope, using your palm, using a crystal ball or using God's Word? That's what Aurora was doing with her Bible when I met her. She was using God's Word the same way a psychic would use the lines on your hand to deliver a spiritual message on God's behalf."

"She's beautiful and she likes me," Daniel said.

"Besides that, she's so upper class in how she acts."

"We're all sinners," Matthew said. "There are no perfect singles in the dating arena. Just because Aurora has a Catholic background and she likes applying Scripture passages from her Bible to other people's lives, it doesn't make her a psychic witch."

"There's one more thing," Michelle said. "Aurora was attributing sensations in her body to the Holy Spirit, as if God was speaking to her through those sensations. For example, if Aurora felt a tingling sensation in her spine, she assumed that something bad was about to happen to her. Or if Aurora felt a stabbing feeling in her heart, that must mean that someone was saying something bad about her."

"You are probably giving her a heart attack right now," Matthew said. "Aurora is probably lying on the ground clutching her heart wondering where the attack is coming from."

"You know I don't like gossip," Michelle said. "We should pray and cover this conversation with God's mercy and grace. I just felt obligated to bring these warning signs to your attention, so if you and Aurora get more serious, you would not only be aware of these issues, but you could help her grow in holiness and break free from any New Age involvement in her past."

"When we get together on Saturday night, I will ask her about any New Age or occult involvement to see where the conversation leads," Daniel said. "Another explanation for Aurora's behaviors could be an authentic movement of the Holy Spirit. In the Book of Samuel, there were several occasions when the Spirit of Yahweh descended upon the prophets, and they would fall into a 'prophetic frenzy,' which would indicate physical sensations, along with the ability to deliver spiritual messages from God."[9]

"I think Daniel and Aurora looked good together," Matthew said. "There were a lot of strange couples at the gallery last night. Did you see the Cuban man with the long circular mustache who was with that young European girl?"

"I gave the young girl in the pink jumpsuit my business card," Michelle said. "We spoke about Jclub and how Christianity was not like other religions, because it's an opportunity to enter into a life-saving relationship with Jesus."

"What about Chester, our friendly art gallery molester?" Daniel asked. "I thought you were going to revoke his membership."

"We are going to file an anonymous police report today," Michelle said. "I have prepared a statement about how young children have been visiting the home of a registered sex offender late at night that we can drop off at the front desk."

"We had better get going," Matthew said. "If Daniel has a hot date with Aurora on Saturday evening, maybe we should prayer walk the strip club on Friday night around eight o'clock."

"We also need to schedule a planning session for the

spring car wash," Michelle said.

"I will be praying for your protection," Daniel said as he got up to leave. "May Yeshua grant you divine favor with the police officers; may the pervert be investigated, arrested and rehabilitated; and may the children in Chester's neighborhood be protected. May Yeshua protect Jclub from all forms of retaliation, and may we avoid any unnecessary encounters with law enforcement in the future."

After Daniel finished his prayer and walked out the door, Matthew asked, "Have you ever considered why the Jewish people have so many reasons not to trust government officials? Just think of all the times they have been oppressed and betrayed by governments around the world. For more than four hundred years, the Egyptians forced the Jewish people into slavery. When they escaped the Egyptian government's oppression, the Babylonian Empire forced them into slavery.

"After they escaped the Babylonian Empire's oppression, they were persecuted by the Roman Empire. Between 1940 and 1944, the Netherlands and Belgium governments passed many anti-Semitic laws. Then we have the German and Polish governments who, under the rule of Hitler, put them in concentration camps for the purpose of eliminating them from the face of the earth."

"It seems very unfair, because the Jewish people are some of the hardest working and most successful people that I know," Michelle said. "I think we should ask

Daniel why the Jewish people are so persecuted and yet remain so resilient."

* * *

"Follow them," a demonic spirit said to his battalion after conducting a reconnaissance mission in the church basement. "I want deceptive spirits to influence the thoughts of our agents at the Paradise Valley Police Department so that when the missionaries file their report it will never get processed. Instill doubt and suspicion into the thoughts of the officer who receives the report. Make the officer very agitated and impatient right before the monkeys arrive."

"What do you want the rest of us to do?" another demon asked.

"Follow them on the highway," the commander said. "Interfere with the vision and thoughts of the other drivers around them in an attempt to cause a fatal traffic accident."

* * *

When the missionaries were getting ready to leave, Matthew started heading in the direction of his silver-colored Toyota 4Runner. After hesitating for a moment he asked, "Do you want me to drive?"

"Is there something about my driving that you don't like?" Michelle asked.

"I love riding around in your Jeep," Matthew said. "Before I bought my 4Runner, I was considering buying a Jeep. I wanted a four-door hardtop, but after adding in all the off-road features, the price was too high."

After Matthew opened the passenger-side door and held it open for Michelle, Overwatch dispatched an assignment of protective angels that formed a defensive barrier around the vehicle. Several of the missionaries' guardian angels were hovering overhead, while another assignment of enforcement angels had been dispatched to the Paradise Valley Police Department.

After driving twenty-five minutes, the missionaries arrived in front of a large commercial building with silver-tinted windows. High above the main entrance, a golden star with seven points that resembled a law enforcement badge displayed the name "Paradise Valley Police Department."

"Do you mind if I wait here?" Matthew asked. "I think you will be more effective and influential on your own."

"I'll be back in a flash," Michelle said.

Inside the front lobby of the police department, three service windows were covered with thick sheets of bulletproof glass. Above each window, a metallic sign displayed the names "Records," "Traffic" and "Criminal" in silver letters.

As Michelle approached the window for criminal complaints, she noticed several surveillance cameras that were mounted on the ceiling, which made her feel a little uncomfortable, as if she were being watched. The officer behind the window was wearing a navy blue uniform with a silver badge, so Michelle approached him and said, "I would like to report a very precarious situation."

"Did an actual crime occur, ma'am?" the officer asked.

"There's a situation that needs further investigation," Michelle said. "Here's the name and address of a registered sex offender who has been luring young children into his home late at night. He may be offering these kids drugs as a way of grooming them for more perverted activities."

"What's your name, ma'am?" the officer asked.

"I would like to remain anonymous," Michelle said. "If you watch this man's house at night after he gets off work, you will see what I'm talking about."

"I will pass this information on to our Special Victims Unit," the officer said. "If the suspect is on probation, or under the supervision of a parole officer, he may be in violation of his release conditions."

"Thank you for your assistance," Michelle said, turning to leave.

When she returned to the 4Runner, she looked around for Matthew, who had been prayer-walking the perimeter of the building. "How did it go?" Matthew asked as he held the door open for Michelle.

"The officer was very professional," Michelle said. "He will pass our information on to a Special Victims Unit that handles cases involving minors. If Chester is on probation or out on parole, there may be conditions of his sentencing that would prevent him from being around minors."

"I'm very impressed by your desire to stand up for

what's right," Matthew said. "I like it when you fight for the oppressed and minister God's love and grace to those who have been hurt."

"Thank you," Michelle said. "I feel better already."

"Although we may never know the results of your actions today, I believe we will have the opportunity to watch movies of every person's life when we get to heaven," Matthew said.

"What do you mean?" Michelle asked.

"Can you imagine watching a movie of Adam and Eve's life? Or watching events from the life of Moses, and then seeing how those events influenced other events in history?"

"I'm hoping there will be a rewind and do-over function for my life," Michelle said.

"In the situation involving Chester, we could see the results of your actions as if you never reported the alleged crime to the Paradise Valley Police Department, and the results of your actions because you did report the crime," Matthew said. "If the police do their job, there may be countless lives that will be changed for eternity, all because you decided to follow Chester home one evening."

"I have always wanted to be a movie star," Michelle said.

"Sometimes it feels like we are all living in an action movie," Matthew said. "Let's use our time and resources wisely to push back enemy lines and advance God's kingdom while there's still time."

"I'm with you one hundred percent," Michelle said as they drove back to the church under the constant protection of the angelic escort.

*   *   *

When Friday evening arrived, Matthew was waiting in the church parking lot with several one-liter bottles filled with holy water. Michelle arrived next, followed by Daniel, who was driving his BMW 7-Series sedan.

"Do you want me to drive?" Michelle asked.

"I think we should take Daniel's car tonight," Matthew said. "It's black and I want to blend in with the night. Besides, that 7-Series has success written all over it."

"We were wondering what makes Jewish people so successful," Michelle said.

"I conducted a little research on Nobel Prize winners when I was in college," Matthew said. "I think you have some explaining to do."

"What do you mean?" Daniel asked.

"There are several categories for Nobel Prize winners, including literature, chemistry, economics, physics, world peace and medicine," Matthew said. "Between 1901 and 2021, there have been over nine hundred Nobel Prizes awarded to individuals and organizations, and over two hundred of those awards have been to Jews. That's an impressive number, but what's even more impressive is the number of Jewish Nobel Prize winners compared to the percentage of Jews living in the world.

"There are an estimated twelve million Jews in the

world, which is less than a fraction of a percent of the world's population. So my question is: How can less than one percent of the world's population win twenty percent of the Nobel Prizes?

"Before you answer that question, let's compare those numbers to the Muslim population. There are over a billion Muslims living in the world, or about twenty percent of the world's population. Because there are only nine Muslim Nobel Prize winners, I'm wondering why twenty percent of the world's population has been awarded nine Nobel Prizes and less than one percent of the world's population has been awarded over two hundred prizes."

"I have a few theories," Daniel said.

"It gets even better," Matthew said. "Jewish Americans are some of the most influential business leaders in the world. Over forty percent of all billionaires in America are Jewish. For example, Larry Page and Sergey Brin, who founded Google, are both billionaires. Dell Computer, Starbucks, Goldman Sachs and Warner Brothers were all founded and owned by Jewish billionaires. In smaller countries, such as Ukraine, there are only four billionaires, but three of those billionaires are Jewish. In addition, all the major banks have chief executive officers who are Jewish, including JP Morgan Chase and Charles Schwab."

"Please tell us your success secrets," Michelle said. "We are all friends here. Wouldn't it be nice if we could be multi-millionaires together?"

After a long period of silence, Michelle looked over at Daniel, who was making a right turn on Franklin Drive and said, "I'm sorry. Are you okay? You look like you are about to cry. Did we say something that was offensive?"

"It's just that for my entire life, my parents have pushed me to be successful, but I don't feel very successful, and I'm certainly not wealthy," Daniel said. "As a Christian, I made a commitment to serve my Lord and Master, Yeshua Hamashiach. There are many warnings in the Bible about how a man cannot serve two masters, and so you see my dilemma. On one hand, I have a family who is constantly pressuring me to become a successful multi-millionaire; on the other hand, I have my Lord and Master telling me that no man can serve two masters."[10]

"I'm sorry, brother," Matthew said. "You are the most successful person I know."

"I respect and appreciate everything you have to say," Daniel said. "There has to be a reason why there are so many Jewish Nobel Prize winners. If we discover the secrets to their success, maybe we can apply these same principles to Jclub."

"That's what I like about you," Michelle said. "You are always turning difficult and challenging situations into a positive and beneficial advantage."

"I will get serious in prayer and ask Adonai to show me why the Jewish people have been so persecuted over the years and yet continue to excel with even greater perseverance," Daniel said. "After Yeshua speaks to my heart, I will share with you all of our trade secrets."

"Let's park in the same place as before," Matthew said as they approached the strip club.

4th CHAPTER

After parking on the hillside, Daniel looked down at the establishment and said, "Last time we were here, the parking lot was full. Now it's half empty."

"Laying down blessed salt is powerful," Matthew said. "I used it at the gym several times to get rid of some people who were polluting the spiritual atmosphere."

"This ought to be a good story," Michelle said.

"What exactly did you put in our water bottles?" Daniel asked.

"Do you remember when the Prophet Elisha used a bowl of salt to purify a well?" Matthew asked.

"It's in Second Kings," Michelle said.

"There was a well that was causing women to have miscarriages," Matthew said. "The water was also caus-ing the land to be unfruitful, and people were getting sick and dying. When the elders of the town asked the Prophet Elisha for assistance, he said, 'Bring me a new bowl, and put salt in it.'[11] After praying a deliverance prayer over the salt, the prophet threw the salt into the well and said, 'Thus says the Lord, I have made this water wholesome; from now on neither death nor miscarriage shall come from it.'[12]

"In that situation, there was an evil presence causing harm and destruction to God's people. Because salt was used as a preservative, Elisha used it to purify the well. In the same way the prophet performed an exorcism on the well using blessed salt through the power of prayer, we are also performing an exorcism on the strip club through the power of prayer."

"You still have not told us what's in the water bottles," Daniel said.

"To make holy water, all you need to do is add blessed salt," Matthew said. "The prayer to make blessed salt comes from the Prophet Elisha when he purified the well. There are many different versions of the prayer, but the one I like using says, 'Almighty God, we ask you to bless this salt as you once blessed the salt scattered over the waters by the Prophet Elisha. Wherever this salt is sprinkled, drive away the power of evil and protect us by the presence of your Holy Spirit.'"

"Did you make your own blessed salt?" Michelle asked.

"Many years ago, I knew a priest who was an excellent preacher," Matthew said. "He had an old Latin rite of exorcism prayer book that contained a prayer for making blessed salt. He offered to bless some salt for me, so I brought him a glass bottle filled with ordinary table salt. When he was praying his exorcism prayers in Latin over the salt, I was also praying my own deliverance prayers in English."

"You never told us what happened at the gym," Michelle said.

"When I work out early in the morning, my gym is usually filled with conservative patriots who just want to be left alone," Matthew said. "Not everybody's a Christian, there are a lot of ex-military guys who just want to pump iron and keep to themselves. Then one day this martial arts guy shows up with a strong demonic presence.

"He was dressed in red silk martial arts pants with Eastern religion symbolism printed down the sides. I tried to avoid him, but he would set up his water bottles and backpack to block off entire sections of the gym that he was using. He also had an unpleasant odor about him that was probably part of his religion."

"What did that smell like?" Daniel asked.

"Maybe it was part of his religion to never wash his body, so he covered over his stench with some kind of detergent-smelling perfume," Matthew said. "That perfume stench got stuck up my nose one day and I couldn't get it out. I could smell him after I left the gym. The guy was demonically oppressed, and he was always doing strange exercises with small weights while chanting mantras to himself.

"Then one day I took a water bottle and added a small amount of blessed salt. Before the gym opened, I prayed and walked around the parking lot three times. I even took my water bottle inside the gym and sprinkled holy water every place where that guy worked out.

"My prayer for the gym was the same as Elisha's prayer for the well. I asked God to drive out everything evil or demonic so the gym could be a community gathering place of conservative patriots who love, support and encourage each other.

"After praying that prayer, that guy never came back. I only saw him one more time at a different club location, so I prayer-walked that building as well. During my prayer time for the second location, I asked God to bind up and destroy everything evil or demonic in the parking lot, so that nothing evil or demonic could enter the building.

"Think of the prayer as a demonic coat check at the front entrance of the building. People who are created in the image and likeness of God are allowed to enter the building and work out, but they are not allowed to bring any of their demonic friends with them."

"I wish we had spiritual eyes to see all the angelic and demonic interactions," Michelle said. "Can you imagine what the parking lot of that gym looked like?"

"After I dedicated both gym locations to the Lord as a spiritually pure environment, I'm assuming God sent an assignment of warring angels to stand guard over the entrance of the property," Matthew said. "Whenever a clean conservative Christian entered the building, there wasn't any problem.

"Whenever a demonically oppressed person tried to enter the building, God's angelic army would arrest the demonic spirits and prevent them from gaining access. I also think this prayer had a profound effect on the homosexuals who used to work out at the gym in the afternoon, because they stopped coming as well."

"What's our prayer strategy for the strip club?" Daniel asked.

"Let's start with a prayer where we take authority over every place the soles of our feet tread," Matthew said. "Because this is our community and the land belongs to God, as God's servants, it's our responsibility to drive evil out of our sphere of influence.

"Because the strip club is no different than the well that was causing miscarriages, we can perform an exorcism by driving out all forms of sickness and death that are causing harm to the patrons who frequent the establishment. In the same way that Elisha prayed over the salt before exorcising the well, we can also pray over our holy water bottles so that wherever this water is sprinkled, the almighty power of God will descend upon the property and drive evil out of our community."

"May Adonai's power be released tonight," Daniel said as he stepped out of the vehicle.

"Let's split up and pray over the outer areas of the parking lot first," Matthew said. "I want to make sure the bouncer doesn't come after us again. If everything seems quiet, then we can move in closer."

"I will cover the west side," Daniel said.

"I'll work the center section," Michelle said.

When Phantalon realized the missionaries had returned and were planning to exorcise the property, he dispatched every demonic spirit under his control to guard the entrance. As soon as the missionaries started taking authority over the property in the name, power and authority of Jesus, Overwatch dispatched an assignment of angels who started cutting the demonic spirits into pieces. There were so many dismembered demonic body parts that were piling up that Overwatch needed to send an assignment of servicing angels to dispose of their remains in the lake of fire. When Phantalon realized the majority of his demonic forces had been annihilated within a matter of seconds, he cried out to his remaining forces, "Pull back immediately!"

While Matthew and Daniel were praying over the parking lot, Michelle approached the main entrance and said to the attendant who was collecting an entrance fee, "Would it be okay to use your ladies' room?"

"This is a club for men," the attendant said.

"I wanted to stop by during the day to speak with the manager," Michelle said. "Is he here tonight?"

"He was in earlier," the attendant said.

"What's your name?" Michelle asked.

"I'm Bruce," the man said.

"Would it be okay to use your ladies' room?" Michelle asked again.

"It's in the back, next to the bar," Bruce said.

When Matthew finished sprinkling all the cars in the

main parking lot with holy water and calling forth an assignment of God's angelic warriors to descend upon the property, he approached Daniel, who was working the west side of the building and asked, "Where's Michelle?"

"I thought she was with you," Daniel said.

"Please don't tell me she went inside the building," Matthew said.

"Let's check around back," Daniel said.

"Hurry, in case she's in trouble," Matthew said as they ran toward the rear of the building.

After Michelle passed the checkpoint where Bruce was working near the front door, she caught the attention of several men who were seated on red chairs in front of elevated platforms with two shiny metal poles the strippers used to keep their balance while dancing.

As she approached a long bar in the rear of the building that was illuminated with soft red neon lights, she unscrewed the cap on her water bottle and turned it upside down, allowing a steady stream of holy water to spill out on the carpet. Once inside the ladies' room, she sprinkled all the walls with holy water before exploring the rest of the club.

After Matthew and Daniel finished searching the entire perimeter, Michelle walked out the front door holding the owner's business card that she received from Bruce.

"Let's go," Matthew said.

"We thought you had been abducted," Daniel said.

"The place is dead inside," Michelle said. "There's nobody around to abduct me."

"What were you thinking?" Matthew asked.

"Haven't you been to a strip club before?" Michelle asked.

"No!" Matthew said as they were walking back to Daniel's car.

"I think we need to pray a cleansing prayer over ourselves," Daniel said, "just in case we picked up something demonic back there."

"I don't feel very spiritual right now," Matthew said. "I'm still angry at Michelle for making us run around the parking lot looking for her."

After the missionaries prayed a cleansing prayer over themselves, Daniel drove back to the church parking lot.

"Are you okay?" Michelle asked as they stepped out of the vehicle.

"We should have anticipated some kind of counter-attack from the enemy," Matthew said. "Let's meet back here Monday afternoon to pray another cleansing prayer over ourselves. Then afterward, we can discuss what happened and make plans for the spring car wash."

After Daniel drove away, Michelle wrapped her arms around Matthew and gave him a long hug. She said in a soft voice, "I'm very sorry. Please forgive me. It won't happen again."

* * *

When Michelle entered the church basement for the Monday afternoon meeting, she said, "What did you want to talk about? I received your text message asking me to arrive early."

"I needed some time to gather my thoughts, so thank you for taking the time to help me work through some issues," Matthew said.

"Sure," Michelle said. "What's up?"

"When most people get angry, it usually comes from being hurt or threatened. So if you want to quickly disarm an angry person, all you need to do is identify the reasons why that person is feeling hurt or threatened."

"In Al-Anon meetings they say, 'Don't work my program, and don't work your own program, but work the Program,'" Michelle said.

"Let me give you an example of how that would work," Matthew said. "Let's say a mother with small children in her car was driving down the street when a drunk driver cut in front of the vehicle and almost caused an accident. The natural response to this situation would be anger, which comes from being hurt or threatened. Although there was no physical damage to the vehicle, there's still the perceived threat of danger, which would cause the threatened mother to become angry.

"In my situation, I was angry with your disappearance at the strip club, but at the time, I didn't know why. After searching my heart to discern why I was so angry, I realized that I was not physically hurt—no physical damage occurred to me or you—but after realizing the dangerous situation you were in, I felt threatened."

"Why were you feeling threatened?" Michelle asked.

"We were going to exorcise a demonic stronghold and we should have been prepared in advance for some kind of retaliation," Matthew said. "As you know, the men who frequent strip clubs have no respect for women, and because those men are already sexually frustrated, there's probably no better place for a woman to be abducted and raped than in the parking lot of a strip club.

"In the same way the mother in the car example loves and cares about her children and wants to protect them from a fatal crash with a drunk driver, I also love and care about you, and I wanted to protect you from being abducted and raped in a parking lot. My other concern was what could have happened if you went inside the strip club asking for a job interview. I'm assuming the girls who work at these places are required to remove their clothes before they're hired. In addition, to removing their clothes for a job interview, who knows what other kinds of perverted activity their employers require.

"When I was running around the parking lot looking for you, I found myself feeling helpless in a dangerous situation. When I couldn't find you, I felt threatened, and when I did find you, the perceived threat quickly turned into anger. After working through my emotions, I wanted to apologize for getting so upset."

"I think it's really sweet that you love and care

about me," Michelle said. "We should have never split up. I should have stayed by your side the entire time. I didn't realize how dangerous the situation was because I felt a sense of empowerment. At first, I thought my feelings of empowerment were being motivated out of love for the women who worked there, but after thinking about the situation some more, it may have been part of the demonic attack."

"What do you mean?" Matthew asked.

"I have also been praying for a deeper insight into what was happening in the spiritual realm," Michelle said. "I believe God showed me two demonic forces that were active at the strip club; one demonic force attacks the men with lust, and the other demonic force attacks the women, making them feel powerful.

"The women who work in strip clubs use their sexuality to seduce men for money. They feel powerful because they can manipulate the weaknesses of men and exploit them for money. I'm wondering if a demonic spirit of empowerment jumped on me, making me feel powerful so that it could lead me into a dangerous situation."

When Michelle was still speaking, Daniel walked down the stairs and said, "I hope I'm not interrupting something important."

"We were just discussing the prayer walk on Friday night," Michelle said.

"How was your dinner date with Aurora?" Matthew asked.

"We went to the Boardwalk Mediterranean Grill so that we could walk around afterward," Daniel said. "I ordered a grilled chicken, black olive and artichoke dish, and Aurora ordered a Greek chef salad. We had a great time and have so much in common."

"I'm so happy for you," Michelle said.

"Were you able to get into some deeper issues," Matthew asked, "about how she came to know the Lord?"

"We spoke mostly about her work as a cosmetics salesperson, and about all the office conflicts she is experiencing with her coworkers," Daniel said. "I was able to ask about her ability to hear from the Lord and deliver spiritual messages to other people on the Lord's behalf, but I felt she was hiding something from me. I was looking directly into her eyes, but then she turned away and her eyes started shifting back and forth. She also denied any New Age or occult involvement."

"What do you think she's hiding?" Michelle asked.

"I'm not sure, but I will keep praying and seeking Yeshua's guidance," Daniel said. "I have also been praying about what makes Jews so successful, and have put together a list of trade secrets that I wanted to share with you."

"That sounds like a great idea for a book," Michelle said. "When can we expect a manuscript?"

"The best part about the trade secrets is that we can incorporate them into our lives immediately," Daniel said. "If you give me a little more time for research, I will be able to share an outline with you next week."

"How about sharing your first trade secret with us at the jazz club on Wednesday?" Matthew asked.

"I will start working on the project right away," Daniel said. "We also need to raise two thousand dollars to pay for the admission fees at the amusement park."

"We need more buckets and sponges this year," Michelle said, "the kind that won't scratch our customer's cars. And don't forget about additional hoses and some Y-shaped adaptors so we can rinse multiple vehicles at once."

"I know where we can get the hoses and buckets," Matthew said. "Is there anything else?"

"We need more money," Michelle said. "Increased memberships, additional donations and a steady stream of revenue would be great. Whatever you guys can do to bring in more income would be greatly appreciated."

"That's why we need the list of trade secrets of successful Jews," Matthew said.

* * *

After the missionaries concluded their meeting on Monday afternoon, Phantalon and his demonic forces tried returning to the strip club, but they were no longer able to access the building or the parking lot because several angelic warriors had been assigned to stand guard over the property. Whenever one of the demonic spirits came too close, an angelic warrior would draw his sword and start a pursuit that would end in the demonic spirit's destruction.

"It's too dangerous," one of the demons said. "Every time we have tried, one of our comrades gets cut up into tiny pieces, and they seal his remains in the lake of fire."

"We need to find another base for our operations," Phantalon said. "I don't want to join forces under the command of another principality, so we had better find an abandoned building that we can use as a temporary base until a better opportunity arises."

* * *

On the day of the car wash, Matthew removed several large wooden signs from the storage room located in the church basement and placed them on the street corner in front of the parking lot entrance. Because the fundraising event had been advertised in the church bulletin, many parishioners stopped by to get their cars washed by the teenage volunteers.

Around ten o'clock in the morning, Father O'Connor arrived and started honking his horn.

"Good morning, Father," Matthew said as he ran over to meet him. "Are you here for a car wash?"

"I have several important meetings today," Father said. "Is there any way you can move me to the front of the line?"

"Just drive your car up front and we will get you washed right away," Matthew said.

After Father O'Connor drove his dark-brown Buick LeSabre to the front of the line, several teenage volunteers washed the outside of the vehicle while

Matthew used a large shop vacuum to clean the carpets and under the seats. "Do you have time for some carnauba wax?" Matthew asked.

"I had better get going," Father said as he drove away in a hurry.

After he left the parking lot, Daniel walked over and said, "He didn't offer to pay anything, so I didn't ask."

"That was a wise move," Matthew said. "We have been using the church's water, electricity and parking lot for free, so the least we can do is bless Father with a free car wash."

5th CHAPTER

At the end of the day, after the teenagers had washed over one hundred cars, a man pulled into the church's parking lot driving an S-Class Mercedes sedan. "Are you here for a car wash?" Daniel asked.

"I wanted to make a donation to support the excellent work that you're doing with the youth," the man said. "Would it be possible to speak with Matthew?"

"He's around here somewhere," Daniel said. "Let me find him for you."

"I'll come with you," the man said as he stepped out of his car and walked toward the front of the line. After recognizing Trevor's father, Matthew greeted him and asked, "How have you been doing?"

"I'm fine, and my business has been lucrative, but my son is going through a difficult time at school," Mr. Baxton said. "He could use some Godly guidance. I wanted to ask for your help because he speaks so highly of you."

"What's going on with Trevor?" Matthew asked. "I haven't seen him at any of our events lately."

"The public schools in Whitmore County have been pushing an LGBT agenda on students, encouraging them to use whatever bathroom they self-identify with, and now my son wants to be a woman," Mr. Baxton said. "He has been hanging out with another boy named Joffrey who has also been a negative influence."

"What can I do to help?" Matthew asked.

"I'm not sure," Mr. Baxton said, removing his wallet from his pocket. "I wanted to make a five hundred dollar donation to help support your ministry."

"I'm very grateful," Matthew said as he reached out to receive the money. "Our goal was to raise two thousand dollars today to pay for the entrance fees at the amusement park next weekend. I'm wondering if Trevor and Joffrey would like to attend as my personal guests. That way, I can spend the day ministering to them to the best of my abilities."

"That would be such a blessing to my family," Mr. Baxton said as he handed Matthew his business card. "You have my work and cell numbers. I will make sure the boys are ready early Saturday morning."

After Mr. Baxton drove away, Matthew approached Michelle and said, "We made our goal!"

"Congratulations," Michelle said. "There are only two more cars in line, so let's close up shop early and celebrate with some Chinese food."

"I will remove the signs and start cleaning up the

parking lot," Matthew said.

By the time the food arrived, all the hoses, electrical cords, vacuum cleaner and wash buckets had been returned to the storage room.

"I'm so tired," Michelle said as she slowly walked down the stairs and into the church basement.

"What did you order?" Daniel asked.

"I made sure everything was kosher," Michelle said, "except for the stir fry rice, which may have some shrimp in it; but don't worry, because I ordered you an extra serving of white rice. In addition, I made sure there were no dairy products or pork in our food. If you want, we can share the Kung Pao chicken, beef with spicy bean sauce and cashew chicken with red peppers."

"Did they give us chopsticks?" Matthew asked.

"Everything is here," Michelle said, "except for some plates from the kitchen."

"I will get them," Matthew said.

After Matthew returned with a stack of dishes, Daniel said, "I have been working on the first success secret that I would like to share with you."

"Please do," Michelle said.

"I have been analyzing the theory that Jews are more successful than other people, but what if the Jewish nation is only average and many Americans have been wasting their true potential?"

"This ought to be interesting," Michelle said.

"Japan is another country that is prosperous, and the students in Japan also have a lot higher intelligence quotients than the average American student," Daniel said. "The question is: What's the difference between Japanese students and American students, or what's the difference between Israeli students and American students?"

"More discipline and motivation," Michelle said.

"The average Israeli child learns three languages before attending grade school—Hebrew, Arabic and English—while the average American only learns one language and spends a lot more time watching television all day. There's also a lot more pressure placed on both Jewish and Japanese students to strive for excellence, to work hard, earn good grades and to be successful.

"Many Jewish parents encourage their children to pursue higher-paying careers in law, engineering, business, banking and finance; while the average American parent allows their children to pursue whatever career path that feels right. Many American college students don't even know what career path they want to pursue, so they sign up for a generic assortment of classes in college."

"Now you're starting to make me feel bad," Matthew said. "I thought you were going to share some success secrets with us that we could apply to Jclub."

"Here's where it gets good," Daniel said. "There's a reason why Japanese and Jewish children have higher IQs than Americans. Part of the reason is the strict discipline of a challenging learning environment, but the other part of the equation is physiological. That's because the human brain is comprised of sixty percent fat, and thirty percent of that fat comes from omega-3 fatty acids. The human body cannot make any omega-3 fatty acids, so that's why they're called *essential*. The best plant source for omega-3 fatty acids is ground flax seeds, and the best animal source comes from fish.

"What's even more interesting is that both Japanese and Israelis eat a lot of fish. Many Israeli mothers intentionally eat a lot of fish during pregnancy and take additional supplements of fish oil, so that their child's brain will develop on the level of a genius.

"Another supplement that has been proven to increase a person's intelligence quotient is iodine. A good example of this comes from the 1920s when the American government started adding iodine to salt because it raised the average American's IQ by fifteen percent. It's also very interesting that the Japanese eat a lot of seaweed with their sushi, and seaweed is extremely high in iodine."

"I remember reading that some of the poorest countries in the world have an iodine-deficient diet," Matthew said. "Do you think there's a connection between iodine deficiency, a lower IQ and financial prosperity?"

"If the only thing a person eats all day is corn, sugar and wheat, they will have an underdeveloped brain with a lower IQ, and they will not be able to excel in higher education," Daniel said. "They will never obtain the highest-paying professions, and those people will never win any Nobel Prizes in chemistry, physics or medicine."

"Now you're making me think about my college friends," Matthew said. "They were more interested in partying and getting drunk than they were in getting good grades. Our modern-day society seems to be more concerned about teaching students the correct transgender friendly pronouns than we are at working hard and striving for excellence."

"That's a summary of an important success secret," Daniel said. "I'm still working on the other aspects."

"That was very informative," Michelle said. "I can't wait to hear about the rest of your success secrets so that we can start applying them to Jclub."

"Let's invite everybody we meet this week to the coffee shop meet and greet on Wednesday," Matthew said. "I would like to sign up ten new memberships."

"We also need to pay the amusement park fees and pick up our day passes," Daniel said.

"I told Mr. Baxton that we would spend the day ministering to Trevor and Joffrey on Saturday," Matthew said. "I will call you tonight with the details so that we can start praying for their healing and deliverance."

* * *

Early Saturday morning, several carloads of Jclub members began arriving at the amusement park near the covered picnic pavilion. While Michelle was busy checking off members' names from a long list, Matthew was handing out the day passes.

After the majority of the tickets had been distributed,

Mr. Baxton arrived in his platinum-colored Range Rover. When the teenage boys stepped out of the vehicle, Matthew said, "Nice ride. You guys know how to make an impression."

Although the teenage boys didn't say anything, they both greeted Matthew with a fist bump.

"We usually ride the biggest roller coasters first with our hands in the air the entire time," Matthew said. "So you have three options to consider: Diamond Back, Phantom's Revenge or Thunderbird."

"Thanks again," Mr. Baxton said as he turned to

leave. "I will meet you in front of the pavilion at six o'clock tonight to pick up the boys." After Mr. Baxton departed and Michelle handed out the last ticket, Matthew asked, "Did you decide on which roller coaster you wanted to ride first?"

"We want to ride Phantom's Revenge," Trevor said.

"There are so many fun rides here," Michelle said. "I want to ride everything, including the Ferris wheel and the merry-go-round. The only ride I don't like is the Tower of Doom. I can't stand the feeling of dangling in the air right before we fall."

After passing through the main entrance, Trevor said, "Come on, Phantom's Revenge is right over there." He was pointing toward a towering configuration of looping yellow tracks that were supported by bright green columns.

After waiting in line for several minutes, Matthew said, "If you want to sit in the front, we will need to get in another line behind those people standing over there."

"Let's go for the front," Joffrey said.

"We will be right behind you," Michelle said as a series of red and black cars arrived on the track.

After rushing down a steep vertical drop, the roller coaster made two upside-down loops before accelerating through a series of twists and turns. After returning to the platform, Matthew said, "What a rush! Let's ride Diamond Back next." As the group made their way through the amusement park toward the red, yellow and purple steel tracks, Michelle said, "There's the Top Speed Dragster and Tilt-A-Whirl."

"Check out those girls over there," Matthew said, pointing in the direction of the bumper cars. "I mean, they're not as good looking as Michelle, and they are way too young for me, but what do you guys think?"

"We're not interested in girls," Joffrey said.

"What's wrong with girls?" Michelle asked.

"Those kind of girls wouldn't be interested in us," Trevor said. "Besides, I'm more gender fluid and Joffrey is gender expansive."

"I don't know what those terms mean," Michelle said. "Will you please explain them to me?"

"It's too complicated," Joffrey said.

"I know what you guys mean," Matthew said. "I watched a video of a non-binary-gender person who was a female, but then that person had an operation to become more gender neutral."

"It's something like that," Joffrey said.

"It was amazing the amount of views this person had on YouTube," Matthew said. "I'm sure this person's Twitter account and Facebook fans were off the charts."

"I want to see how many views," Joffrey said as he removed his cell phone from his pocket.

"I'm not sure I could find the video again," Matthew said. "I don't remember the Twitter handle, but I can tell you, most of those views were fake."

"What do you mean by *fake*?" Joffrey asked.

"If you search the Internet using the key words

'social media marketing,' you will find many companies that will provide a thousand Facebook likes for only ten dollars," Michelle said.

"You can also get a thousand YouTube views for six dollars," Matthew said. "Come on, Diamond Back is right around the corner. We need to keep moving if you want to ride everything before six o'clock tonight."

Because Trevor and Joffrey were using their cell phones to search the Internet for social media marketing companies, Matthew took a seat on a nearby park bench. Michelle sat down beside him and started praying for a breakthrough. When the boys finished searching the Internet, they looked up as if bewildered, so Matthew said, "Can we ride Diamond Back now?"

After everybody walked in silence for several minutes before reaching a long line that had formed in front of the roller coaster, Matthew said, "There's a big difference between real-life reality and the enhanced reality of the virtual universe. The gender-neutral person in the video may seem like a social media celebrity with millions of views and thousands of positive comments, but in real life, the video was very difficult to watch."

"Why do you say that?" Trevor asked.

"Before I share with you what I watched on the video, let me explain how easy it is to manipulate social media accounts," Matthew said. "There's an estimate that forty percent of Twitter accounts are bots. The same is probably true with Facebook and other social media companies.

"When a politician wants to get reelected, he will negotiate a multi-million dollar contract with Facebook and Twitter. In exchange for the money, the social media executives will program the bots to promote the politician, and then they will program other bots to destroy the repetition of the opposing candidates.

"The same technology works when a political party wants to promote the latest LGBT agenda. Some very wealthy people in the world want to use their money to undermine traditional Christian values and promote the LGBT agenda in schools. To do this, they find a video of a gender-fluid person who had an operation and then they turn loose the positive comment bots. Immediately after posting the video, the gender-fluid person will receive thousands of positive likes from all over the world, with comments such as, 'Way Cool,' 'Great job,' 'You look fab' and 'Love the new look.'

"All these positive comments may make the person who posted the video feel like a rock-star celebrity in the enhanced virtual reality universe, but in real life, it's a very different scenario."

"What happened in the video?" Joffrey asked.

"It was a video of a topless woman who had an operation so she could look more like a man. This person did an excellent job at getting a male haircut that looked great. The problem was that this person had two, six-inch-long horizontal scars across her chest where her breasts used to be. When I watched the video, you could tell this person still had a woman's body."

"That's so cool," Joffrey said.

"The scars across this person's chest were bright red and still very fresh. They were a half-inch thick. If I saw this person with a group of guys playing football on the beach, everybody would know this person was a woman. That's because a woman's body is different than a man's body.

"Let's use Michelle as an example," Matthew said as he reached out for her hand.

"No touching," Michelle said.

"When a woman is knit together inside her mother's womb, she is created by the Spirit of God with two X chromosomes inside her cells," Matthew said. "These chromosomes give a biological woman a different bone structure than a man.

"For example, look at my neck. Do you see my Adam's apple? Now look at Michelle's neck. It's totally different. My hands are bigger and stronger. Women have a higher percentage of body fat than men, and it makes their skin soft and smooth. I would be happy to show you guys my muscular legs, but they will never look as gorgeous as Michelle's legs."

"Hey, no touching," Michelle said.

"You could tell the person in the video was a biological woman because she still had a slender female waste. She still had soft skin. She is never going to have a big, strong muscular chest with broad shoulders because she doesn't have any Y chromosomes.

"The saddest part of the video is that this person

will never experience authentic acceptance in the real world. If this person took off her shirt to play football on the beach with a group of guys, they would instantly know that something was wrong.

"They would look at her soft female skin, and see the gruesome scars across her chest where her breasts used to be. They would notice her slender female waist, and they would instantly know that this was a female who desperately wanted to be a male.

"She may be the greatest hit on social media with a billion views and thousands of positive comments, but in real life, she is going to be treated like an outcast."

"My dad's a doctor, and he can prescribe hormones to help gender-fluid people make a smoother transition," Joffrey said.

"It's true that men have more testosterone and women have more estrogen, but hormone treatments will never change how men and women were created by God inside their mother's womb with X and Y chromosomes," Matthew said. "If you give a biological female heavy doses of testosterone, it may interfere with her menstrual cycle, but she will still have menstrual cycles.

"If you give a man heavy doses of estrogen, he will lose muscle mass and will not have the strength or stamina to accomplish hard physical labor. So if you really want authentic love and acceptance in the real world, you guys have to stop running in the wrong direction, turn around and go the opposite direction."

"What do you mean?" Trevor asked.

"Beautiful women are naturally attracted to masculine men. If you want a beautiful woman's love and affection, you need to be more masculine, not more feminine. Instead of asking your father for estrogen to be more like a woman, you should be asking for testosterone to be more like a man. That way, you guys could hit the gym, pack on thirty pounds of upper body strength, and the girls would be all over you."

"I think you are both very handsome young men," Michelle said.

"You do?" Trevor asked in a soft voice.

"God created you as men because he has a purpose and plan for your lives," Michelle said. "Instead of rebelling against God, and fighting against God's will for your lives, you should seek after God and cooperate with his plans. When you work in partnership with God, you will be able to achieve incredible accomplishments with your lives."

"It looks like we're next," Matthew said as Joffrey pressed against the turnstile and entered the loading platform for Diamond Back.

"Let's sit in the middle section," Michelle said before she climbed into a bright red, bullet-shaped car.

After the attendant made sure all the passengers were securely fastened in their seats by an overhead U-shaped harness, the cars pulled forward with an abrupt snap and started climbing a steep ascent. Upon reaching the top, the cars paused for a brief moment before speeding through a series of twists and turns. After the ride came to a screeching halt back at the platform, Michelle said, "I think we should call Daniel and Aurora to see how they are doing with the younger members."

"If you guys will excuse us for a moment, we need to make a phone call," Matthew said. "We will be right over there."

After walking away from Trevor and Joffrey to make a phone call, Matthew said, "I think we should tell them about all the regrets men experience after having a sex change operation, along with the devastating and permanent consequences they would experience if they had their genitals removed.

"It would also be great if you could keep affirming and validating their masculinity. Did you see how they reacted to a woman's love and attention? It seems like they never received their mother's love, and you have the perfect opportunity to fill that void in their hearts with a few kind words of encouragement."

"I will do my best," Michelle said.

6th CHAPTER

After spending the day ministering to Trevor and Joffrey at the amusement park, Matthew received a call on his cell phone from Mr. Baxton. "I'm sorry, we lost track of time," Matthew said. "Give us about ten minutes to reach the pavilion because we are on the opposite side of the park."

"Why do we have to leave so early?" Joffrey asked. "The park closes at ten o'clock."

"Mr. Baxton set the time," Matthew said. "Let's hurry because we're already late."

When the group arrived at the pavilion, Mr. Baxton was pacing back and forth while talking on his cell phone. Upon seeing Trevor, he ended the call and said, "Did you boys have a good time?"

"It was great," Trevor said. "We rode every ride except the Tower of Doom."

"I wanted to thank you again," Mr. Baxton said, shaking Matthew's hand.

"It was my pleasure," Matthew said. "I wanted to

invite you and Trevor to work out with me at the gym sometime. I'm there early morning, three days a week. I think it would be a great blessing for Trevor and Joffrey, especially if they want to try out for the football team next year."

"I'll think about it," Mr. Baxton said. "I'll be out of town next week, but I will call you when I return to discuss the details."

After Mr. Baxton drove away, Michelle called Daniel to see how he was doing with the younger members of Jclub. After a brief conversation, she ended the call and said, "All the parents have picked up their children except for Jenny's mom, who will be here at seven o'clock. I asked Daniel if he wanted to join us for dinner, but he already made plans with Aurora."

"Do you want to go back inside?" Matthew asked. "We could pick up some burgers and ride a few more roller coasters before closing."

"I'm feeling a little too old for this," Michelle said. "With all that bouncing around, my back is starting to hurt. It's also going to be difficult to find healthy food in there. How about we go to my house and I will make dinner?"

"That sounds great," Matthew said. "Let's call Daniel and Aurora to tell them we are leaving."

* * *

Michelle lived with her mom in a Victorian-style, two-story home located about three miles away from Holy Trinity Catholic Parish. Large oak trees surrounded

the property, and throughout the well-maintained landscaping areas, there were many wildflowers and thriving rose bushes.

After parking his 4Runner behind Michelle's Jeep in the driveway, Matthew stepped out of his vehicle and said, "You have such a beautiful home. I love the size of your back yard and that huge garage. You could probably fit four cars in there."

"The previous owners used to store a sailboat in there," Michelle said as she unlocked the back door.

"Is your mom home?" Matthew asked.

"I don't think so," Michelle said. "She usually spends Saturday evenings at her friend's house playing cards and socializing with members of her Bible study group."

"What's for dinner?" Matthew asked.

"I have been trying to eat more healthy," Michelle said. "I have wild salmon, and I can make a large salad with French bread."

"That sounds great," Matthew said. "Do you need any help? You know how much I love to cook."

"If you want to grill the salmon, I will prepare the salad," Michelle said.

After the food was ready, Matthew and Michelle took seats at the outdoor dining table underneath the covered back porch. Michelle lit an antique oil lamp and placed it in the center of the table. "Will you please say grace?" Michelle asked as the flicker of the lamp illuminated the young couple with a soft glow.

"Heavenly Father, we thank you for the day, and we ask you to bless this meal and our conversation this evening. Please continue ministering to Trevor and Joffrey. Watch over every word that was spoken today. Prevent the enemy from stealing any of the seeds that were planted. May every seed of truth that was spoken today be firmly rooted in the fertile soil of their minds, so that your truth will grow, mature and produce a rich harvest. In the powerful name of Jesus we pray."

"Beautiful prayer," Michelle said as she served the salad. "For the salad dressing, I have been using condensed orange juice that I buy in the frozen food section. It's sweet and tangy and has only one ingredient."

"It tastes great," Matthew said. "I like the fact that there's only one ingredient. When the label has a block of text with words so complex that nobody can pronounce them, you know it's loaded with harmful chemicals and preservatives."

"I have been researching what Daniel told us about omega-3 fatty acids," Michelle said. "As it turns out, they are very difficult to incorporate into your diet."

"Is that why you are serving salmon tonight?" Matthew asked.

"I was going to make dinner for my mom, so I bought the wild-caught salmon," Michelle said. "Do you know what they do to farm-raised salmon?"

"I heard that farm-raised salmon is so sick and unhealthy that the fish's flesh would be a dirty gray color," Matthew said. "That's why they add a pinkish-orange dye to the fish's food in an attempt to color the entire fish pink from the inside out. This also explains why the packaging says 'color added.'"

"There's probably less omega-3 fatty acids in farm-raised salmon than in wild-caught salmon because of the fish's diet," Michelle said.

"Did you know they also feed farm-raised salmon the cheapest industrial waste they can find?" Matthew asked. "All those toxins build up in the fish's flesh, and we wonder why Americans are experiencing an ever-increasing amount of cancer year after year."

"I have been researching the most economical way to incorporate more omega-3 into my diet," Michelle said. "It's not going to be easy, because even though peanuts are high in fat, they contain no omega-3 fatty acids. The same is true for almonds. One cup of avocado has twenty-two grams of fat but only a tenth of a gram of omega-3 fatty acids. The best plant source would be flax seeds, which contain thirty-two grams per cup."

"How many cups of avocados would you have to eat to receive the same amount of omega-3s as one cup of flax seeds?" Matthew asked.

"That's a good question," Michelle said as she reached into her pocket to pull out her cell phone. "Thirty-two grams in one cup of flax seeds versus two-tenths of a gram in one cup of avocados. According to my math, a person would need to eat one hundred and sixty cups of avocados to equal the same amount of omega-3 fatty acids found in one cup of ground flax seeds."

"Why do flax seeds need to be ground?" Matthew asked.

"They also need to be refrigerated," Michelle said. "When God created flax seeds, he gave them an extremely hard shell that the human body cannot digest. This super-hard shell protects the valuable omega-3 fatty acids from deterioration, so the best way to consume them is by keeping raw seeds in the refrigerator. Then right before you eat them, place several tablespoons of seeds in a coffee grinder and make a powder that can be added to fruit smoothies. You can also add water to the ground flax seed powder to make a peanut-butter-style paste."

"How many omega-3s are in salmon?" Matthew asked.

"Eight ounces of wild salmon contains two and a half grams of omega-3 fatty acids, which is about the same as sardines," Michelle said. "One cup of walnuts contains ten grams of omega-3 fatty acids, but there's a difference between animal sources and plant sources."

"What's the difference?" Matthew asked.

"Something about the length of the fatty acid chains," Michelle said. "Because plant sources are more economical, I was going to start with organic flax seeds at four dollars per pound, along with some walnuts at six dollars per pound. I will also incorporate wild salmon into my diet once or twice a week."

"My grandparents used to take a spoonful of cod liver oil every day, and they never suffered from Parkinson's, Alzheimer's or any other neurological or cognitive disorder," Matthew said.

"I also wanted to research krill oil supplements," Michelle said. "Although it would be more convenient to take fish oil capsules, if the manufacturer heats the fish oil to burn away the fishy taste, the heat will also destroy the molecular structure of the omega-3 fatty acids, so the best way to consume them would be through natural food sources."

"Did you also research iodine?" Matthew asked.

"We could eat more seaweed with our sushi," Michelle said. "Maybe a better option would be nascent iodine, which is the purest molecular form of iodine that you can buy in liquid drops. There's also a mixture of nascent iodine, potassium iodine and sodium iodine that comes in liquid drops."

"I heard the lack of iodine causes hair loss and creates havoc on a person's hormones," Matthew said. "It's also essential for healthy thyroid function, which regulates a person's weight."

"I'm going shopping next week," Michelle said. "I will let you know what I discover."

After enjoying a long conversation on a variety of topics, Matthew said, "Thank you for dinner this evening and for the great day. You're such a blessing to me. You did an excellent job ministering to Trevor and Joffrey by affirming and validating their masculinity. I can't thank you enough."

"It was my pleasure," Michelle said. "I will continue praying for God to set those young men free from the devil's bondage of gender-identity confusion."

"Let's meet at the church Tuesday morning to discuss how we can provide our members with more spiritual growth," Matthew said. "We should also discuss the advertising campaign for the Candlelight Jazz Club."

* * *

Early Tuesday morning, Matthew unlocked the church basement doors and began making a pot of Earl

Grey tea. When Daniel and Michelle arrived, he greeted each of them with a hug and asked, "How was your weekend?"

"It was great," Michelle said. "How was your time with Aurora?"

"It was fine," Daniel said in a soft voice.

"Just fine?" Matthew asked. "Please share some details."

"After the amusement park, we went back to Aurora's apartment for dinner and a movie," Daniel said.

"Then what happened?" Matthew asked. "It feels like you are holding something back."

"I'm not sure Michelle would understand," Daniel said.

"You know how much I love and respect you," Michelle said. "You can share anything with me in total confidence, knowing that I would never tell another person."

"I'm a little embarrassed to say this, but when a man lusts after a woman, he should expect to reap what he has sown," Daniel said. "He should expect to experience sexual feelings, but what happens when a man hasn't been lusting, and a spirit of lust comes on him from an external source?"

"When you say external source, do you mean a demonic attack?" Matthew asked.

"It's very strong," Daniel said. "I know what it's like to lust, and when I commit the sin of lust, I can expect sexual thoughts to enter my mind. When I engage in sexual thoughts, I should expect to feel sexual feelings in my body.

"I'm experiencing the same effects of lusting in my body, except I'm not lusting. I could be completely alone by myself, totally focused on writing computer code, then all of the sudden, out of nowhere, a powerful sensation of sexual feelings for Aurora will come over me."

"I'm wondering if Aurora has been praying some kind of love spells on you," Michelle said.

"That would make a lot of sense," Daniel said. "If I were lusting after Aurora, I should expect to reap the consequences of what I have sown and feel sexually excited. If I block all those thoughts from entering my mind, and refuse to make any agreements with sexual spirits of lust, and a powerful sexual spirit still comes over me, then it has to be coming from an external source."

"That's why we need to incorporate more Bible study programs and fellowship groups into our Jclub events," Matthew said. "I think we should make it a mandatory requirement for all Jclub members to attend at least one Bible study meeting per week."

"If we make it a mandatory requirement, we may lose members," Michelle said. "In addition, we would have an uncomfortable enforcement issue to deal with."

"If we start losing members, we will also lose revenue," Daniel said.

"I agree that we need more spiritual growth

workshops, fellowship groups and empowerment seminars, but we can't force an authentic relationship with God on anybody," Michelle said. "If we make it a mandatory requirement, it will only drive people away."

"Let's add two weekly Bible study groups to the schedule," Matthew said. "They don't have to be mandatory, but let's place a greater focus on the spiritual growth of our members."

"I think we need to add some self-improvement seminars into our schedule," Michelle said. "Members like Trevor and his friend, Joffrey, are not going to show up for a weekly Bible study group, but they might attend a self-empowerment seminar. We know that authentic self-empowerment can only come through Christ, so if our seminars are going to be powerful and effective, they need to be based on an authentic relationship with Jesus."

"I like the idea of a spiritual empowerment seminar," Daniel said. "If Aurora and I attended a seminar, it would give us the opportunity to discuss the content afterward, which could lead to more involvement with the fellowship groups."

"I think we need more of God's healing power in the seminars," Michelle said. "We don't need another chat room where participants discuss the theology of deliverance; we need the power of God to transform our lives so that those who attend the event will be forever changed."

"What did you have in mind?" Matthew asked.

"How about an emotional healing seminar where we can work through past issues that have been causing problems in our present-day relationships?" Michelle said. "I have a few unresolved issues regarding my father's death that I could be working through. Trevor and Joffrey have some kind of issues regarding women. Maybe they never received their mother's love and support when they were little boys, and now they want to become more like women in an attempt to receive more love and support from women."

"Or maybe they never received their father's love, validation or approval, and now those inner wounds are being confused with the LGBT agenda that's sweeping across our nation," Matthew said.

"I'm not sure what's going on deep inside their hearts, but we have an all-powerful, loving God who wants to heal our broken hearts and transform our lives," Michelle said.

"How do you propose that we incorporate God's healing power into a two-hour seminar?" Matthew asked.

"It's going to take a lot of prayer," Michelle said. "I would suggest placing yourself in an empty white room. Pretend there's nothing in this perfectly white room except for you and God. Once you are ready to embrace the hurt and pain from your past, the next step would be to give God permission to bring up some issues.

"For example, maybe there's something about your ex-fiancée that is causing problems in your present-day relationships. After you ask God how he wants you to resolve those issues, spend some time listening for the answers. If you and God can work through those issues within two hours, then you could incorporate those same techniques into a two-hour seminar."

"I'll schedule some prayer time with God inside the empty white room," Matthew said. "We also need to pray for Daniel's sexual purity before we leave."

After Michelle put away the cups and dishes that were used for the mid-morning snack, she placed her hands on Daniel's shoulders and began to pray.

Matthew stood by her side and continued the prayer by saying, "Dear Lord Jesus, we come before you sinful in great need of your healing and forgiveness. Please forgive us for all the times we have fallen short of your holy standard of perfection. Please wash us clean with the blood you shed on the cross of Calvary for the forgiveness of our sins.

"We ask that you send forth an assignment of angels to strike down and destroy anything evil or demonic that has been attacking our brother, Daniel. Please purify his sexuality and break all love spells and incantations off him. We ask this through Christ our Lord."

"Thank you," Daniel said. "I feel better now."

"When you were praying, I felt a sense of urgency that the Lord wants Daniel to discern and discover the underlying source of this attack," Michelle said. "We know this attack is coming from the devil, but what is giving the devil the right to operate in your life?"

"I'm not sure," Daniel said. "I will seek Yeshua's guidance."

"Let's invite everybody we know to the jazz club on Thursday night," Matthew said as he picked up his jacket. "I also want to promote our new Bible study groups at all our events."

* * *

The Candlelight Jazz Club was located near the state capital building across the street from the federal courthouse. It was a popular meeting location for young attorneys and political activists during the day, but because the weekday evenings were less crowded, Michelle was able to reserve twenty tables on the upper terrace for Jclub members.

When Michelle arrived with two new friends, she approached the club's owner and said, "Bonjour, Anthony, I would like to introduce you to Sabrina and Kristine. They are both graduate students from Stanford Medical."

"It's a pleasure to meet such beautiful women," Anthony said as he removed a box of candles from behind the bar. "We had a last-minute cancellation, but our replacement band is a high-energy saxophone crew called Benevolence."

"Can we help with the candles?" Michelle asked.

"That would be great," Anthony said as he handed Sabrina a lighter.

The Candlelight Jazz Club was illuminated with purple wall sconces and burgundy-colored stage lights

that reflected off the surfaces of the shiny black tables. The flickering lights that were placed inside the crystal candleholders provided the club with an intimate setting for deeper conversations.

After Michelle and her friends finished lighting all the candles, they took a seat in the upper terrace overlooking the stage. "We want to incorporate more spiritual growth workshops into our events," Michelle said.

"What kind of workshops?" Kristine asked.

"The president of Jclub wants more fellowship groups and personal-empowerment programs," Michelle said. "If we could find several other women from the medical profession who wanted to meet once a week, that would be a perfect opportunity for you to develop deeper friendships, while at the same time receiving more prayer support. We also wanted to incorporate more self-improvement seminars into our Jclub events to help members achieve their ultimate potential in life."

"Both of those options sound great," Sabrina said.

"Here comes our president now," Michelle said as she introduced her friends to Matthew.

"It's good to meet such lovely ladies," Matthew said. "This is Omar. He's an account executive with First National Bank & Trust."

After Matthew greeted Michelle's friends, he said, "Omar was telling me about all the Old Testament passages that are mentioned in the Quran. It was so fascinating that I can't wait to hear the rest. So if you ladies will please excuse us, we will be right over there."

7th CHAPTER

After Matthew and Omar moved to the opposite side of the room, they took a seat at an empty table. Matthew continued his conversation by saying, "There are so many beautiful women at Jclub, but the majority are very serious Christians, which may be a big problem for a Muslim man."

"There's no problem at all," Omar said. "Muslim men are allowed to marry Christian women so long as they convert to Islam."

"Another option would be for you to convert to Christianity," Matthew said.

"That would be unlikely to happen," Omar said.

"I'm interested in learning more about the Quran," Matthew said. "From my understanding, it was written in the sixth century by the Prophet Muhammad, who traveled around as a caravan trader. During his journeys, he compiled religious teachings from both Christians and Jews into a holy book for the people living in Saudi Arabia."

"That's essentially correct," Omar said. "The Quran contains many passages of Scripture that are mentioned in both the Old and New Testaments of your Bible."

"Can you give me some examples?" Matthew asked.

"The story of creation, the conflict between Cain and Abel, and the account of Noah's ark are all referenced in the Bible and the Quran," Omar said.[13] "In addition, there's the destruction of Sodom and Gomorrah, the narrative about Jonah and the whale, and how Joseph forgave his brothers after he was sold into slavery."[14]

"What New Testament passages are referenced in the Quran?" Matthew asked.

"The Quran contains many passages regarding the life of Isa and his virgin mother, Maryam," Omar said.[15] "In addition, many of Isa's miracles have also been recorded in the Quran."[16]

"That's so interesting because the majority of the Old Testament was written hundreds of years before Christ was born," Matthew said. "In the third century, Pope Damasus commissioned Saint Jerome to produce a Latin version of the Bible—so he translated the Hebrew Scriptures, along with the Gospels and letters written by Saint Paul to the newly established churches—and compiled them into one book. Then three hundred years later, the Prophet Muhammad quotes from both the Old and New Testaments in the Quran."

"What's your point?" Omar asked.

"If the Bible existed hundreds of years before

the Prophet Muhammad was born, I'm wondering if the Quran mentions the sources where all those Old and New Testament Scripture passages came from?" Matthew asked.

"The Quran confirms the authority of the Scriptures many times," Omar said. After removing his cell phone from his pocket, he began searching for information that had been posted on his favorite Islamic website.

"Can you give me an example?" Matthew asked.

"In the second surah, the Quran says that we 'Believeth in Allah and His angels and His Scriptures and His messengers. We make no distinction between any of His messengers.'[17] Then in the fourth surah, the Quran says, 'Believe in Allah and His messenger and the Scripture which He hath revealed unto His messenger, and the Scripture which He revealed aforetime. Whoso disbelieveth in Allah and His angels and His Scriptures and His messengers and the Last Day, he verily hath wandered far astray.'"[18]

"If the Quran confirms the authority of the Scriptures, and if the Prophet Muhammad quoted Bible passages that existed hundreds of years before he was born, how can you deny the Gospel message?" Matthew asked.

"Because your version of the Bible is corrupt," Omar said. "Allah would never allow one of his servants to suffer a painful and humiliating death on a cross as the Roman crucifixion."

"How can you say our Bible is corrupt when it's the

same Bible that existed in the sixth century?" Matthew asked. "The Bible that existed when the Prophet Muhammad wrote the Quran is the same Bible that we use today. When the Quran confirms the authority of the Scriptures that existed in the sixth century, it also confirms the authority of the Scriptures that we use today, because both the sixth-century Bible and our modern-day Bible are identical."

"I don't know how to respond to that analogy," Omar said.

"There's no need to respond," Matthew said. "You have succeeded in making me very interested in reading sections of the Quran that confirm the authority of the Scriptures. Why don't you work on the answers to my questions while I download a PDF version of the Quran from the Internet to conduct more research."

"*Inshallah*," Omar said. "I have enjoyed our time together. *Allah ma'ak.*"

After Matthew excused himself from the table, he looked around the club to see if he could locate Daniel, who was seated on the main level with Aurora. After approaching the table, he said, "Do you mind if I join you this evening?"

"Please have a seat," Daniel said.

After greeting Aurora, Matthew said, "I wanted to ask your advice about incorporating more spiritual growth workshops and personal empowerment seminars into our Jclub events."

"That sounds very interesting," Aurora said.

"I wanted to make attendance to either a Bible study group or a fellowship group mandatory for all Jclub members, but Daniel didn't think it would be a good idea," Matthew said.

"I attend a weekly prayer group," Aurora said.

"I didn't know that," Daniel said.

"It's called Our Blessed Mother's Handmaids, and we meet on Saturday mornings in honor of Our Lady of Medjugorje," Aurora said. "We usually start by praying the rosary, and then our members read their favorite prophetic messages that they received during the week. We usually conclude by praying for our personal needs."

"How many of your members have visited Medjugorje?" Matthew asked.

"Almost everybody," Aurora said. "We try to make a pilgrimage to Medjugorje once a year."

"Have you visited other apparition sites?" Matthew asked.

"I have been to the Basilica in Mexico City where the Virgin of Guadalupe appeared to Juan Diego," Aurora said. "I have also visited Fátima, where Our Lady of the Holy Rosary appeared to Lúcia, Francisco and Jacinta, as well as Holy Love Ministries in Maranatha Spring. I have also visited the Queen of the Holy Rosary Shrine in Necedah, Wisconsin, where the Mother of God appeared to Mary Ann Van Hoof."

"It sounds like you would be in favor of a prayer group or fellowship attendance for Jclub members," Matthew said.

"I love my prayer group," Aurora said. "The Blessed Mother is so powerful. She always comes through for me and gives me everything I ask for in my novenas."

"Thank you for your assistance," Matthew said. "I appreciate your perspective."

"I'm so happy that I could help," Aurora said.

"I had better check on Michelle before it gets too late," Matthew said. "Let's meet at the church tomorrow morning around nine o'clock."

* * *

The next day, when Daniel and Michelle walked down the stairs and into the church basement, Matthew turned to Daniel and said, "You are in so much trouble."

"What happened?" Michelle asked.

"I don't want to talk about it right now," Daniel said.

"Does this have something to do with Aurora?" Michelle asked.

"Let's not talk about it right now," Matthew said. "If you and Daniel want to discuss it after our meeting, that would be fine by me."

"It's a good thing I brought one of Daniel's favorite delicacies this morning," Michelle said. "I picked up a dozen bagels at the bakery, but when I went to the grocery store, I purchased Brie cheese instead of cream cheese."

"Thank you very much," Daniel said.

"I wanted to make some blackberry tea, warm up

the Brie in the oven and top our bagels with melted cheese and pear slices," Michelle said.

"There were eighty-three members who attended the jazz club last night," Daniel said. "The owner appeared to be happy with the turnout, so I thought the event was a success."

"It was a great night," Matthew said. "I had an incredible conversation with Omar about Islam, and I can't wait to hear about those new friends of yours."

"I met them on campus several weeks ago," Michelle said. "We were talking about setting up a medical student fellowship group. Sabrina seemed very interested, so I decided to share the Gospel message with them. I started with a verse from Saint Paul's letter to the Romans where it says, 'To one who works, wages are not reckoned as a gift but as something due.'[19]

"Then I asked Sabrina and Kristine to combine the meaning of that verse with another verse from Saint Paul's letter to the Romans that says, 'For the wages of sin is death.'[20]

"Instead of saying the penalty for sin is death, I thought it sounded better to say that God does not punish us with the death penalty when we sin, but that death is something we have earned, something that we are entitled to receive.

"Because we are all sinners, I presented my friends with the possibility of receiving what they have already earned. The other option would be to surrender their lives to Jesus, so that he could pay the death penalty on their behalf. It was a simple choice to make: Do you want to pay the death penalty yourself, or do you want Jesus to pay the death penalty on your behalf?

"Because Sabrina and Kristine both came from religious backgrounds, it was an easy choice to make. We bowed our heads while the saxophone player was pouring out his heart into the music, and we prayed a prayer of surrender. We surrendered our lives into Jesus' service and asked to be filled with the Holy Spirit so that we could accomplish God's will in our lives."

"That's a beautiful testimony," Matthew said.

"Now it's your turn," Michelle said. "When I looked over at you and Omar, it appeared as though you were both engaged in a very serious conversation."

"Don't worry," Matthew said, "I'm not going to sell Omar a Jclub membership because he's a very serious Muslim. I met him at the bank several weeks ago, and he was very helpful and friendly. I could feel the Holy Spirit wanting me to reach out to him, so I invited him to several events. I'm surprised he called me yesterday afternoon and chose the jazz club, because Muslims don't drink alcohol and they don't go to bars."

"What were you talking about that was so serious?" Michelle asked.

"Muslims are very serious about their religion," Matthew said. "Any time you discuss religion with a Muslim, it's going to get intense."

"Does he speak Arabic?" Daniel asked.

"I don't know," Matthew said. "He was coming

from a place of religious superiority with me as if Judaism were a grade school education, Christianity a high school education, and Islam a college-level education. He was talking about how the Bible speaks of fasting, yet the majority of Christians don't fast. I didn't want to argue with a man who fasts from sunrise to sunset during Ramadan without eating or drinking anything, so I just listened to what he had to say."

"Is there anything we should be praying about?" Michelle asked.

"I'm feeling a spiritual connection with Omar and would like to meet with him again," Matthew said. "I also downloaded a PDF version of the Quran and searched the document for the word *surrender*."

"Why did you choose that word?" Daniel asked.

"Muslims consider themselves to be surrendered servants of Allah," Matthew said. "There's a verse in the Quran that says, 'Religion with Allah is the Surrender to His will and guidance.'[21] Before a Muslim man can surrender his life to Allah's will and guidance, he first needs to be able to hear and discern God's will and guidance for his life. That means Muslims have to be open to accomplishing God's will in their lives, and to do that, they will need spiritual guidance from God, which only comes from listening to the softly-spoken voice of the Holy Spirit."

"That's not going to be possible without the infilling of the Holy Spirit," Michelle said.

"If Omar were filled with the Holy Spirit, then I

would say his religion would be college level," Matthew said. "One of the major problems with Islam is that Muslims have never accepted Jesus' sacrifice on the cross for the forgiveness of their sins. Because sin separates humanity from God, Omar has never received the gift of the Holy Spirit, and without the Holy Spirit, he is never going to receive God's guidance. Without God's guidance, he will never accomplish God's will in his life."

"Maybe we could help Omar by revisiting some lessons from his elementary school education," Daniel said.

"Now let's look at how this concept applies to Christians," Matthew said. "If the proper way to pray is by surrendering our lives unto God's service, then we should be aligning our will up with God's will. We acknowledge that reality in the Lord's Prayer when we say, 'Your will be done, on earth as it is in heaven.'[22]

"If the healthy way to pray is by aligning our will with God's will, then the unhealthy way to pray is telling God what we want, and then expecting God to give us whatever we want. When some Catholics pray to God and don't get what they want, they will start praying to an assortment of spiritual entities that will give them anything they want. A vast majority of these spiritual entities have been appearing at false apparition sites throughout the world."

"I'm thinking this has something to do with Aurora," Michelle said.

"Maybe we should stop the conversation right now,

because I don't want to get angry and say something that I will regret," Matthew said. "I want you to know, Daniel, that I love you very much, and I need some time to examine my heart, because every time I get angry, it comes from being hurt or threatened. Because you're my best friend, I don't want to see you get hurt, and it hurts me to see the pain that you are about to experience."

Because Daniel remained silent and looked as if he were about to start crying, Matthew said, "If you and Michelle would be so kind as to excuse me, I would like to leave now. I have an appointment with a potential donor this afternoon."

"Let me walk you out," Michelle said as she followed Matthew up the stairs.

"What's up?" Matthew asked as he approached his 4Runner.

"I wanted to schedule some time with you to discuss marketing for the emotional healing seminar," Michelle said. "Because we don't have any events on Saturday, I was wondering if you would like to stop by my house for dinner."

"I appreciate the invitation," Matthew said. "Instead of putting you through the hassle of shopping and meal preparation, what if I took you out to a nice restaurant on Saturday night? There's a new place that I wanted to try called the Hideaway Chophouse."

"That sounds very fancy," Michelle said. "Are you asking me out on a date?"

"I'm not sure," Matthew said. "You know that I have a difficult time trying to define that word, so let me make reservations and I will pick you up around seven o'clock."

* * *

Later that week, when Matthew arrived at Michelle's house on Saturday evening, he was planning to greet Michelle's mom if she was home; but before he could step out of his 4Runner, Michelle had already locked the front door and was walking toward his vehicle. She had her strawberry-blonde hair tied back with a bow and was wearing a short, black cocktail dress with matching high-heel shoes.

"Does this outfit look okay for the Chophouse?" Michelle asked.

"You look incredible," Matthew said.

"I have another outfit ready if you think I should wear something more business savvy," Michelle said.

"I'm the one who needs to change," Matthew said. "You're making me look bad—as if I should be wearing something more formal."

8th CHAPTER

The Hideaway Chophouse was located in an upscale area of the waterfront district on Thirteenth Avenue. The main dining area consisted of semi-circular booths that were grouped in the shapes of four-leaf clovers and were separated by large palm trees that produced even more privacy.

After being seated in a booth with an incredible view of the waterfront, Michelle looked at the menu and said, "Would you please order for me tonight?"

"Let's share several side dishes," Matthew said.

After looking through an elegantly designed and very expensive menu, Matthew said, "I would suggest the grilled maple sea bass or the lamb chops with fresh mint. I'm going with the eighteen-ounce porterhouse. Because our dinners include a complimentary house salad, we could share a sweet potato casserole with pecan crust and the grilled asparagus with hollandaise sauce."

"The maple sea bass sounds delicious," Michelle said as their waitress approached the table.

"I have been struggling with marketing ideas for the healing seminar," Michelle said. "I don't know what to call the event, and I'm concerned Jclub members will not understand the importance of emotional healing. If they knew what was involved, they might not want to attend."

"Why do you think they might not want to attend?" Matthew asked.

"I have observed a lot of resistance in Al-Anon meetings from people who will do anything to avoid working on their issues," Michelle said. "There's all kinds of clichés they sling around during meetings, like 'We are only as sick as our secrets' and 'It works if you work it.' In expectation of the resistance, I was thinking about a focus on Unpacking Your Partner's Bags, because everybody is interested in fixing other people's problems, but very few people want to invite God's love and healing power into their own traumatic past experiences. Another option would be to call the seminar the Mystery Healing Event, or the BYOB Party, which could stand for 'bring your own baggage.'"

"Let me share with you what I have so far," Matthew said. "I wanted a very solid Christian foundation for the seminar because I don't want anybody to say that it's New Age or based on secular psychology. Although the Bible doesn't give us a list of instructions for emotional healing, it does speak about forgiveness. When Jesus was teaching his disciples how to pray, he said, 'If you forgive others their trespasses, your heavenly Father will also forgive you; but if you do not forgive others, neither will your Father forgive your trespasses.'"[23]

"There's also the parable about the king who settled accounts with his slaves," Michelle said. "After the king forgave one slave the equivalent of millions of dollars, the same slave refused to forgive his fellow servant the equivalent of a few hundred dollars. When the king found out about it, he turned him over to be tortured until he paid the entire debt. Then at the end of that parable, Jesus said the same thing will happen to every one of us unless we forgive our brothers and sisters from the heart."[24]

"Because Sacred Scripture provides a very solid foundation regarding our need to forgive people who hurt us, we could start the seminar with the forgiveness process, and then transition into what happens when we are hurt in the past but were too young to know how to forgive," Matthew said.

"Can you give me an example?" Michelle asked.

"I was thinking about a little boy who was playing in the grass with his toy trucks and got stung by a bee. I'm sure the little boy would start crying and run to his mother for assistance. If his mother were full of God's love, she would be able to pick up the child and explain to him what happened.

"God's love would flow through the mother's heart and into the child's heart, and through a deeper understanding of the event, along with the reassurance that he was going to be okay, the little boy would be able to work his way through the forgiveness process. He would be able to forgive the bee colony along with the individual bee for stinging him, and afterward, he could return to the grass and continue playing with his toys.

"Now let's look at what would happen if the little boy never received the love and support he needed from his mother, and all that hurt and pain got repressed deep down in his heart. Maybe his mother was an alcoholic who was drunk when the little boy was stung. If that were the case, she would probably blame him, or maybe tell the child that it was his own fault.

"If the mother were really drunk, maybe she would start laughing at him, or tell him to stop crying, or even punish him for crying. If the little boy never received the love and support that he needed to work through that traumatic past experience, all that hurt and pain would get repressed deep down in his heart, and it would affect his God-given natural programming.

"When we see an adult who is terrified of bees, we know that person was not born with the fear of bees. A tiny baby doesn't even know what a bee looks like. God doesn't create babies with an inherent fear of bees, so when we see a man or woman who is terrified of bees, we know that person encountered a painful experience in the past and has never worked his or her way through the healing and forgiveness process."

"Let me see if I understand what you are saying,"

Michelle said. "If the lack of forgiveness can change our God-given natural programming and cause problems in our present-day relationships, then by working our way through the forgiveness process, we should be able to restore our God-given natural programming and eliminate those problems from our present-day relationships."

"Maybe it's not such a big deal if your relationship partner is scared of bees, but what about a gambling addiction or a pornography addiction?" Matthew asked. "A young child is not born with an inherent tendency to lose all of his or her money in Las Vegas at the high-stakes poker table or view images of naked humans on the Internet. We are created in the image and likeness of God, so if your relationship partner has a gambling or pornography addiction, we know that it's a direct result of something that happened to that person in the past.

"The same concept would apply to all our relationship issues. God doesn't create verbally abusive babies, or critical, manipulative and controlling babies. All those tendencies are acquired from a person's past; and through the power of forgiveness, we have the opportunity and ability to be set free."

"I love it," Michelle said. "There are so many people who attend Al-Anon meetings that I would like to invite to this seminar. It feels like we have the power to break the underlying bondage that drives almost all addictive behaviors. My only question is how do you plan to get participants to open the doors of their hearts to receive the fullness of God's love, so that they can be set free?"

"I'm not sure," Matthew said. "I have been spending time in the empty white room with God, but I keep thinking about Omar. There are millions of Muslims in the world who are extremely serious about their religion. The Quran confirms the authority of the Scriptures, and yet they have never accepted Jesus' sacrifice on the cross for the forgiveness of their sins."

"I already posted the 'Mystery Healing Seminar' online last week," Michelle said. "That only gives us thirteen days to prepare."

"I'm sure we can fill the church basement with hurting people," Matthew said. "I'm also sure that God's healing power will be present during the seminar to enter into people's hearts so that they can be set free. All we need is a mechanical mechanism that allows people to open their hearts, embrace the hurt and painful events from their past, and invite God's love and healing power into their lives."

"Maybe we could use a written letter exercise to help participants express their feelings, something similar to a journaling technique," Michelle said.

"That's a great idea," Matthew said. "I will experiment with a written letter exercise while spending time with God in the empty white room; but please tell me your thoughts about ministering to Muslims."

"I don't know much about Islam," Michelle said, "except that some women are extremely oppressed. In many countries, Muslim women are treated like second-class citizens. Some of the women are not allowed to leave their homes without a male escort, and others are not allowed to attend school. Many women are forced to wear a burka, or a full-length body gown with a veil to cover their face."

"Ever since I read about the life of Saint Paul, I wanted to be a traveling missionary," Matthew said. "I'm sure you know the passage where Saint Paul received a stoning from the Jews. He was beaten with rods, shipwrecked for a night and a day, and imprisoned; he went through many toils, hardships and sleepless nights, yet he still kept on going.[25] Everybody knows Saint Paul was unstoppable, but my question is: What motivated him to suffer all that abuse and still keep going?"

"I'm sure he had a serious calling on his life," Michelle said.

"What if everybody has a serious calling on their lives, yet very few Christians want to surrender their lives into God's service?" Matthew asked.

"Why do you think Saint Paul suffered all that abuse and still kept going?" Michelle asked.

"I think he was driven by his love for lost souls and the excitement of adventure," Matthew said. "I think Saint Paul was so consumed by the Holy Spirit that he didn't have a choice. If the Holy Spirit prompted Paul to deliver the Gospel message to a group of angry witch doctors, he would be fully confident knowing that if

God had a purpose, he would also have a plan, and if God had a plan, he would have God's protection at all times. I think Saint Paul's love for God, and his love for lost souls, was a greater motivating force than any amount of fear for his own safety.

"I also think that Saint Paul was driven by all the miracles he experienced, but unfortunately, I don't think we will experience that kind of outpouring in our modern-day American churches."[26]

"Why do you say that?" Michelle asked.

"When the ministry situation is very challenging, it seems that God moves with a greater magnitude of power. That's why I like the idea of ministering to Muslims in Africa. Because Muslims are so serious about their religion, it would be very easy to engage them in a spiritual conversation. At the opposite extreme, there are so many complacent people in America who have grown cold and indifferent to religious matters. Because of our wealth and prosperity, many people in America just don't care about religious matters, and their apathy makes it very difficult to reach lost souls.

"Besides, I like traveling and have always wanted to visit Africa. It seems like a perfect match—traveling the world as an evangelist for Christ while moving with the miracle-working power of God."

"That's an impressive vision," Michelle said.

"Do you like traveling?" Matthew asked.

"I have always wanted to travel the world," Michelle said. "I like the adventure of exploring new places and the thrill of wanting to see what's around the next corner."

"I never knew that about you," Matthew said. "I never thought you would be willing to leave all your friends behind."

"We could stay in touch through social media," Michelle said. "Besides, it would allow me to make new friends in other countries."

"Would you like some dessert or coffee?" Matthew asked. "They have French silk pie, crème brûlée, salted caramel cheesecake or tiramisu."

"No sweets for me," Michelle said.

"Eating sugar is way too addictive for me," Matthew said. "Once I start eating sweets, it messes with my appetite, and I start craving more. It has always been easier to avoid sugar altogether."

"It's getting late," Michelle said. "Are you ready to go? We have a lot of work to accomplish before next week."

* * *

On the day of the seminar, one hundred and thirty Jclub members gathered in the church basement. Twenty rows of cafeteria-style tables had been set up facing the stage, and each table contained a stack of notebook paper, pencils and a box of tissues.

Matthew started the seminar by saying, "I would like to share with you a story about a man named Jack. When Jack was a little boy, his older brothers and sisters were playing a game in the basement called 'Let's see who will fit inside the trunk with the lid closed.' When it was Jack's turn, his siblings lowered the lid and locked him inside. Because the kids didn't have a way to open the lock, they went back upstairs, turned off the basement lights and forgot about him. Jack was locked inside that trunk for hours. It was dark, and he was having a difficult time breathing. He thought he was going to die.

"When Jack's mother came home from work that evening, she realized that one of her children was missing, and that's when the oldest brother remembered that Jack was still locked inside the trunk. Everybody rushed to the basement to let Jack out, and by God's grace, the little boy was still alive.

"I don't have all the details on how Jack's mother helped her son recover from this traumatic experience, but from that point forward, Jack started suffering panic attacks. As an adult, a paralyzing grip of anxiety would come over him at the worst possible moment, and it would cause serious problems in all his relationships. It got so bad that Jack was on the verge of getting a divorce because his wife couldn't deal with his emotional issues any longer.

"If Jack were here with us today, how would we help him? We know Jack was created in the image and likeness of God, and that God doesn't create little children with a subconscious desire to experience panic attacks. We also know that if Jack wasn't born with panic attacks, those issues must have originated from a source, usually from some kind of traumatic past experience.

"In Jack's situation, it is very easy to discern the source of his panic attacks, but maybe there are some Jclub members in the audience today who are experiencing a similar type of relationship problem or emotional issue, except that they don't know how to identify the source. That's okay, because we have an all-knowing, all-powerful, infinite loving God who is here with us today. He is ready to bring everybody in this seminar the healing that we need.

"If Jack were here with us today, the first step in the healing process would be to ask the Holy Spirit to take Jack back into his past to show him the root cause of his panic attacks. All Jack would need to do is close his eyes, pray for guidance and give the Holy Spirit permission to bring up some issues from his past. Once the Holy Spirit showed Jack the source of his panic attacks, the next step would be to go back in time to complete the forgiveness process.

"When this event occurred, Jack was way too young to know how to work his way through the forgiveness process. His mother was probably too busy making a living, and she probably never took the time to help her son heal. Because Jack was never able to work his way through the forgiveness process, all those negative emotions became repressed deep down inside his heart and changed his God-given natural programming, causing him to experience his present-day anxiety attacks.

"It would have been nice if Jack's mother had conducted a family meeting and allowed Jack to express all his negative emotions. The little boy would have probably started crying, telling his brothers and sisters how dark it was inside the trunk, how he couldn't breathe and how he felt abandoned and betrayed by his own family members.

"If Jack were allowed to vent all of his negative emotions, it would have been helpful if his family members took turns expressing their love for him and apologizing for their reckless actions. If this type of family meeting had occurred, Jack would have been completely healed, but because this family meeting never occurred, all those negative emotions got trapped deep down inside Jack's heart.

"If Jack were here with us today, we would allow him to express all of his negative emotions. We would want Jack to vent all his anger, fear and feelings of betrayal. After Jack released all his negative emotions, the next step would be to replace those negative emotions with the love, support and encouragement that he needed but never received.

"As Christians, we have a more advanced step that we can use, because we can invite the healing power of Jesus into our traumatic past experiences. Just imagine what would happen if that little boy invited Jesus into the dark trunk to keep him company. Because Jesus is the Light of the World, I'm sure the Lord would have illuminated the darkness inside the trunk with his brilliant light.[27] The presence of Jesus would have been there to keep him company.

"Although Jack never invited Jesus into the trunk as a little boy, he has the opportunity to invite Jesus into his life and heart today. Jack can invite the healing power of Jesus into his most painful past experiences and ask God to transform those situations into an everlasting blessing.

"If Jack were here with us today, I would ask him to get very serious in prayer and ask the Holy Spirit to show him something from his past that needs healing. Once he identified an issue, he would need to conduct a family meeting to vent all of his negative emotions and allow his family members the opportunity to express all of the love, support and encouragement that he deserved to hear but never received. To complete the healing process, we would invite Jesus into our hurtful past events and allow his miracle-working power to transform our negative past events in a way that will bring us the greatest amount of eternal blessings.

"Because this is a sacred process, I wanted to begin with a prayer by asking God to build a canopy of protection around this room. Picture the canopy as an invisible barrier, similar to bulletproof glass, where we invite the Blessed Trinity inside the canopy to minister to everyone in this room. We also want to ask God to send an assignment of angels to stand guard over us, so that there won't be any distractions. So if you are ready, please close your eyes so that we can pray together."

After Matthew called down a canopy of protection to surround the church basement, Michelle released the pause button on the compact disk player and started playing soft, instrumental music.

After the prayer, the majority of the participants sat in their chairs motionless as if deep in thought. Then one by one, the Jclub members began writing. Some of the participants started scratching heavy, angry words into the paper, while others wrote longer sentences and started crying. The emotional healing seminar lasted for almost two hours, and at the end of the service, there was a pile of used tissues on every table.

When everybody had finished working through a negative past experience, Matthew returned to the stage, picked up the microphone and said, "The next step in the healing process is to share your letter with another person. This step is optional, so you are free to leave at any time, but I would encourage you to break out into small groups and share the loving words that you deserve to hear with another person."

After Matthew made the announcement, a few of the participants gathered together the pages of their healing journal and headed for the door. Then one by one, people started moving chairs around so they could socialize with their friends. Before long, the entire church basement was filled with the joyous sound of friends interacting with each other. The time for sharing lasted another hour, and at the end of the evening, everybody was emotionally exhausted.

When Matthew was rolling up the microphone cord, Michelle approached him and said, "That was excellent! The miracle-working power of Jesus was so profoundly evident this evening."

"I'm surprised everybody broke out into smaller groups," Matthew said. "I thought they would be running for the door."

"That was such a blessing for me," Daniel said as he approached the stage.

"I would like to share my healing letter with you," Michelle said.

"Can we get together tomorrow evening?" Matthew asked.

"I have my women's Bible study group during the day and the roller skating event at night," Michelle said.

"I'm meeting with a wealthy donor on Sunday, but we haven't decided on a time," Matthew said. "He's interested in funding short-term mission trips. How about we meet back here Monday morning at nine o'clock?"

* * *

After the demonic spirits finished searching the city for an abandoned warehouse that they could use for their base of operations, they reported back to Phantalon and said, "We have identified several opportunities for your consideration."

"Did you find another strip club that we could control?" Phantalon asked.

"All the strip clubs in this city are under the influence

of rival principalities," one of the demons said. "A few of the leaders from those principalities said we could join their operations, but you would no longer be a ruler over us."

"What are the other options?" Phantalon asked.

"We found several magicians who would be willing to sell their souls into our possession if we help them perform magic tricks," another demon said.

"I don't like it," Phantalon said. "I want something more sinister."

"We found a group of Satanists who are hungry for more power," another demon said. "They are working with a rival principality, but we may be able to over-power them and take control of their operations."

"Give me more information," Phantalon said.

"They have two young girls who live on a farm outside the city limits," the demonic spirit said. "They are using the girls as breeders, so they can perform both animal and human sacrifices. They celebrate the Black Mass, engage in sexual orgies and have several govern-ment officials who are members."

"That sounds like a perfect opportunity," Phantalon said.

9th CHAPTER

Early Monday morning, when Daniel unlocked the doors of the church basement, he began making cinnamon tea. A few minutes later, Michelle arrived and helped him cut up a pineapple and set out cups and dishes. By the time Matthew arrived, everybody was ready to start the meeting, so Matthew began in prayer. After discussing several Jclub business matters, he said, "Who wants to go first?"

"When we prayed for the Holy Spirit to bring up a negative past experience, I had so much anger at my father that I didn't know where to begin," Michelle said. "My father was an alcoholic, and he had been drinking before picking up my sister from soccer practice. I never had a chance to say goodbye, so in my imagination, I pictured my sister in heaven with Jesus.

"She looked so happy and peaceful that I could feel the Lord wanting me to forgive my father, so I pictured him standing next to Jesus. I started writing all the reasons why I felt hurt, abandoned and betrayed by his careless actions. I told him how he destroyed our family and how he devastated my mother's life. After releasing all my angry emotions, I started writing an apology letter on my father's behalf.

"Because my father was standing next to Jesus in a completely healed state full of God's love, I started writing all the loving words that I needed to hear. After my father apologized for devastating our family and causing me so much pain, I could feel the Lord encouraging me to forgive him and focus my attention on running the race with perseverance.

"The Scripture passage that came to mind was when Saint Paul spoke about athletes who discipline themselves to compete in a race. The athletes endure hardships to win a perishable wreath, but in our case, we have the opportunity to compete for an everlasting reward for all eternity.[28] I know I have more work to do, but this seminar was a major breakthrough for me."

"That's so beautiful," Matthew said as he leaned over to hug Michelle.

"I wrote my letter to Yeshua apologizing for my inappropriate behaviors with Aurora," Daniel said. "I asked Yeshua if I had his permission to date Aurora, and he said 'No!' After realizing how far I had wandered away from Adonai's protection, I broke up with her the following day. I also wanted to ask for your forgiveness, because I know how much stress and anxiety the relationship has caused you to experience."

"'As far as the east is from the west, so far he

removes our transgressions from us,'" Michelle said.[29] "There's nothing left to forgive. We love you and didn't want to see you getting mixed up in a sinful situation."

"I also asked Yeshua the question that you asked me several weeks ago," Daniel said. "I think the sexual feelings of lust were coming on me from Aurora's prayer group."

"Oh, you think so," Matthew said.

"The devil had the ability to attack me because I stepped outside of Adonai's will for my life," Daniel said. "I never asked Yeshua's permission to date Aurora, and I most certainly did not have Yeshua's permission to engage in any kind of sexual activities with her. The relationship was in direct conflict with Sacred Scripture when Saint Paul spoke about being unequally yoked by saying, 'Do not be mismatched with unbelievers.'"[30]

"Am I missing something here?" Michelle asked.

"I never told you, but when we were at the jazz club, I asked Aurora if she wanted to join a Bible study group," Matthew said. "Aurora told us she was involved with a Marian prayer group, and that many of the members have visited numerous apparition sites. She also said the Blessed Mother gives her everything she wants."

"After leaving the jazz club that evening, I started researching the names of the apparition sites that Aurora had visited," Daniel said. "Many of them have been condemned by the Catholic Church, which doesn't make sense to me. Why would a conservative Catholic girl visit controversial apparition sites when there were so many negative reviews online?"

"Let me break it down for you," Matthew said. "In Aurora's defense, I'm sure she doesn't think she was doing anything wrong. It's the Catholic Church's fault for not providing better teachings on the healthy way to pray in communion with the saints to God, and the unhealthy way of praying directly to a vast assortment of spiritual entities in an attempt to get anything you want.

"A good example of the healthy way to pray in communion with the saints to God comes from Sacred Scripture and our own prayer lives. For example, when Saint Paul wrote his letter to the church in Ephesus, he addressed it to the 'Saints who are in Ephesus and are faithful in Christ Jesus.'[31]

"A good definition for the word *saint* are those who have been sanctified and set apart for God. According to the *Catechism of the Catholic Church*, the Church is the holy people of God and her 'members are called saints.'[32] According to that definition, we are all saints. So the healthy way to pray in communion with the saints to God is for us to bow our heads, close our eyes and pray together directly to God.

"It would be inappropriate if I started praying to Michelle as if she took the place of God. We can pray together to God, or I can ask Michelle to pray for me, but the *Catechism* makes it very clear that all prayer needs to be focused on God, and that any prayers that are not prayed in the name of Jesus have no access to God."[33]

"Then why do Catholics pray to Mary?" Michelle asked.

"Once we understand how the saints on earth can pray together to God, we can apply the same concept to the saints in heaven, because we are all one family," Matthew said. "The Bible speaks about a great cloud of witnesses in the Book of Hebrews, along with a group of martyrs in the Book of Revelation, who are constantly offering prayers of intercession on our behalf.[34]

"Picture Abraham, Isaac and Jacob along with Peter, Paul and John standing before God's throne, interceding on our behalf. Then imagine what it would be like to join our prayers together with their prayers as we all pray together to God. That's the official teaching of the Catholic Church, but the problem is no one understands the proper way to pray in communion with the saints to God.

"When Catholics don't understand the proper way to pray in communion with the saints to God, they can very easily fall into the sin of idolatry. When they start praying to all kinds of spiritual entities that have been appearing at false apparition sites, it's very easy to open the door to the demonic. I'm sure that many Catholics have spent countless hours asking God for something that was not in their best interest. Instead of spending time practicing contemplative prayer, and learning how to listen and discern the softly spoken voice of the Holy Spirit, they start praying to the Blessed Mother in an attempt to get whatever they want.

"If the Blessed Mother doesn't answer their prayer requests immediately, they will start praying to the Black Madonna. If the Black Madonna doesn't give them what they want, they start praying to Our Lady of Lourdes, or Our Lady of the Americas or Our Lady of Emmitsburg."

"Do you think Aurora's prayer group was praying to all those spiritual entities on my behalf?" Daniel asked.

"That would explain the mysterious sexual attacks that would come on you out of nowhere for no apparent reason," Matthew said. "Aurora probably went to her prayer group and told her friends how she met this kind, good-looking, intelligent guy at the art gallery and that she wanted to make him fall in love with her.

"Upon receiving Aurora's prayer request, the members of that group probably started praying to the Gospa of Medjugorje, the Immaculata or the Queen of Heaven that's mentioned in the forty-fourth chapter of Jeremiah.[35]

"Because the prayer team members were not praying to God in Jesus' name, their prayers had no access to God. Because the prayer team members were probably committing the sin of idolatry, Satan's vast army of fallen angels would have access to those prayer requests in the same way they would have access to the intentions of a New Age witch."

"Instead of calling it witchcraft, maybe we should call it Marian-craft," Michelle said.

"What's the difference between a group of witches who pray to the Ascended Master Mary or the members of Aurora's prayer group who pray to the Gospa? If a witch invoked a love spell by praying to the Gospa, asking that Daniel fall in love with Aurora, then demonic spirits would go forth and attempt to make him fall in love with her, probably by plaguing him with sexual sensations all day long."

"That's exactly what it felt like," Daniel said.

"I think we should pray another cleansing prayer over Daniel," Michelle said. "The Scripture verse that comes to mind is from the First Letter of Paul to the Corinthians, 'The body is meant not for fornication but for the Lord.'"[36]

"I didn't have sex with Aurora," Daniel said.

"Even though you didn't have sexual intercourse with her, I still want to break all sexual soul ties," Matthew said as he stood up to pray. "Heavenly Father, we thank you for our brother, Daniel. Please descend upon him with your healing power. We know from your Word that when a man lusts after a woman, it's the same as committing the sin of adultery with her.[37] We also know from your Word that sexual intercourse has been reserved for marriage and that we are required to keep our marriage beds pure and undefiled.[38]

"We also know from your Word that sexual sins have the power to bond two people together.[39] Because it's not your will that Daniel be bound together with Aurora, we ask you to break all unhealthy soul-ties in the name, power and authority of Jesus. If Daniel has taken any part of Aurora's heart, we ask you to remove those parts from him right now, purify and cleanse Aurora's heart, and restore them to her in the name of Jesus."

"Will you please pray to break the soul ties in your own words?" Michelle asked.

"Yeshua Hamashiach, I am very sorry for getting involved with Aurora," Daniel said with his head bowed toward the ground. "If I have interfered with any aspect of Aurora's sexuality or taken any part of her heart, I release those parts to you right now. I ask you to purify and cleanse every aspect of Aurora's heart and restore them to her. In Yeshua's name I pray."

After a moment of silence, Michelle said, "If Aurora has interfered with any aspect of Daniel's heart, or taken any aspect of his sexual purity away from him, we ask you to remove those aspects from Aurora, purify and cleanse them, and restore them to Daniel in the name of Jesus."

"Thank you for your powerful prayers," Daniel said. "When I was dating Aurora, a demonic covering of darkness came over me. It was so thick, I couldn't work on the Jewish success secrets; but after I broke up with her, I could feel the darkness lifting off me and the Holy Spirit returning back into my life."

"Does that mean you will be sharing the rest of your success secrets with us?" Michelle asked.

"I will work on them this week," Daniel said.

"I wanted to put Daniel in charge of the art galley on Friday night," Matthew said.

"What's going on Friday night?" Michelle asked.

"I wanted to visit a mosque, and I was hoping you would come with me," Matthew said.

"I was planning on meeting several new members at the art gallery on Friday," Michelle said.

"Friday is an important day for Muslims," Matthew said. "Jews celebrate the Sabbath on Saturday, Christians celebrate the Lord's resurrection on the first day of the week, and Muslims conduct a prayer service in the mosque on Friday. I wanted to ask some questions about Islam, tell them we are interested in learning more and see how they treat us."

"Do I have to wear a full-length burka?" Michelle asked.

"I'm sure you can find some stylish Muslim fashions online," Matthew said. "If you wear long pants, a long-sleeve jacket and a headscarf, with shoes that are easy to remove, I'm sure you will be fine."

* * *

When Friday afternoon arrived, Matthew drove over to Michelle's house and parked in the driveway behind Mrs. Nobility's pearl-colored Honda Odyssey. Michelle and her mother had been waiting under the shade of the covered porch drinking tall glasses of mint tea. "Good afternoon, Mrs. Nobility," Matthew said. "How have you been doing?"

"I'm doing fine," she said, "thank you for asking. My daughter told me you were planning to visit a mosque this evening, and I found myself a little concerned for your safety."

"This mosque seems more community-friendly than other mosques in the area," Matthew said. "They even advertise an open-house event on their website. I tried calling the phone number several times, but it only goes to a recording."

"How do I look?" Michelle asked as she twirled around to show off her wide-legged, charcoal-colored pants, white blouse and reddish-brown checkered jacket.

"You always look great," Matthew said.

"I have two scarves to choose from," Michelle said, holding one up in the air to cover her hair.

"I like the rose-colored, floral design," Matthew said.

"That's my favorite too," Mrs. Nobility said.

"Don't worry, Mom," Michelle said, "everything will be fine. I will call you with an update once we arrive."

After kissing her mother, Matthew and Michelle drove away as Mrs. Nobility waved goodbye.

"You have such a sweet mother," Matthew said.

"She will probably stay up all night praying for our safety," Michelle said. "Please remind me to call her with an update once we arrive."

"I watched some online videos about the proper etiquette for visiting a mosque," Matthew said. "In some countries, women are not allowed to enter the mosque, but at this location, they have a women's section and a men's section, so it looks like we are going to be separated all evening. We also have to take our shoes off at the door, and make sure you never walk in front of a man when he is praying, because it will void his prayers."

"Are you serious?" Michelle asked.

"That's what the video recommended," Matthew said. "Keep in mind that we are dealing with religious people who have never been filled with the Holy Spirit."

"Similar to the Pharisees who killed Jesus," Michelle said.

"That's an excellent comparison," Matthew said. "The Pharisees needed to observe hundreds of religious rules and regulations in order to please God, so all their focus was on the external practice of religion. They were so busy practicing religion that they failed to enter into an authentic relationship with Jesus. They never accepted Jesus' sacrifice on the cross for the forgiveness of their sins, and they were never filled with the Holy Spirit."

"If the Pharisees who killed Jesus and the Muslims who have been known to kill Christians share the same hardness of heart, how do you plan to minister to them?" Michelle asked.

"Saint Paul ministered to the Pharisees by entering the synagogue on the Sabbath, and he used the Jewish Scriptures to prove that Jesus was the Messiah," Matthew said. "In the same way, we are about to enter a mosque on Friday and share with them what the Quran says about the Messiah."

"This should be an interesting learning experience," Michelle said. "Let me see if I understand you correctly.

We are going to be separated in different sections. We haven't been invited to speak at the mosque. They don't know we are coming, and somehow, through the power of God, we are going to hijack a Friday evening prayer service to tell them about the Messiah."

"That's an excellent idea," Matthew said, "except I didn't want to stay for the prayer service part."

"How long are you planning on staying?" Michelle asked.

"Muslims pray five times a day: once before sunrise, midmorning, afternoon, sunset and after dark," Matthew said. "When Muslims are not praying at these specific times, the mosque is open to the community for personal prayer, spiritual reflections and social interaction.

"Because we are going to arrive between the afternoon prayer time and the sunset prayer time, the mosque should be open for visitors who want to learn more about Islam. All we need to do is act very respectful, ask a lot of questions and make some new friends."

10th CHAPTER

After removing their shoes, Matthew and Michelle walked through the main entrance of the mosque. There was a sign in the lobby that listed the location of the main prayer hall, men's ablution and women's ablution.

"It looks like your washroom is down that hallway," Matthew said.

As Michelle was walking toward the women's section, Matthew approached two men in the lobby and said, "*Assalamu alaikum.*"

"*Wa'alaikum assalam,*" the men said.

"I have a few questions about the Quran that I was hoping you could answer," Matthew said.

"*Inshallah,*" one man said. "May Allah's will be accomplished. My name is Asad, and this is my brother, Jamal."

After introducing himself, Matthew said, "The Quran speaks about the leader of the devils many times. In surah twenty-three, it says that Iblis can incite humans to sin by whispering to their hearts.[40] The Quran also

says that Iblis can make evil suggestions and teach men sorcery.[41] My question is: How can a devout Muslim man protect himself from shaitan's power?"

"Because the Quran says that Allah is our protector and provider, we do not need to worry about shaitan's power," Asad said. "All we need to do is pray five times a day and lower our gaze when we encounter a woman."

"That's easier said than done," Matthew said.

"Because the meaning of the word *hijab* describes a barrier, it applies to both men and women," Asad said. "When we encounter a woman who is not wearing the hijab, we can create a barrier by lowering our gaze."

"I need to work on that," Matthew said. "The devil is very good at tempting men to commit the sin of lust, but what happens when Iblis influences our religious leaders' minds and hearts for the purpose of leading their congregations astray?"

"Why would you say that?" Asad asked.

"I was reading the Bible about Jewish religious leaders who were called *Pharisees*," Matthew said. "These men were very serious about practicing a form of religion that was pleasing to God, but they were obviously under the devil's influence. The devil was able to harden these men's hearts and prevent them from accepting the gifts of the Holy Spirit."[42]

"Because the Quran repeatedly asserts Allah's absolute oneness, I'm wondering what you mean by the 'Holy Spirit'?" Asad asked. "Allah would never share any of his divine attributes with another deity."

"The Quran states in surah sixty-six that 'Mary, daughter of Imran, whose body was chaste, therefor We breathed therein something of Our Spirit. And she put faith in the words of her Lord and His Scriptures, and was of the obedient,'"[43] Matthew said. "We also know from the Quran that Mary gave birth to Isa, whom the Quran describes as the Messiah.[44] Because the Quran describes Isa as the Messiah eleven times, I'm thinking this declaration has a great deal of importance.[45] My question is: What does the word *messiah* mean in Arabic?"

"I do not know," Asad said as he removed his cell phone from his pocket. "Let me check an official source."

After spending several minutes visiting various sites hosted by Islamic scholars, Asad said, "The word *messiah* is associated with Isa Al-Masih, which means Jesus Christ or the Anointed One."

"That's very interesting," Matthew said. "If Maryam was a virgin whose body was chaste, and if Allah breathed something of his Spirit into Mary's body so that she could conceive and give birth to Isa the Messiah, and if Isa the Messiah promised to send the power of the Holy Spirit into the lives of all true believers, then shouldn't all true believers want to receive the power of the Holy Spirit?"

"*Inshallah*," Jamal said.

"I was hoping that you guys would pray for me so that we could receive the power of the Holy Spirit," Matthew said. "Will you please pray with me?"

"Why do you want to receive power from the Holy Spirit?" Asad asked.

"I want the power of the Holy Spirit in my life to provide spiritual protection from the devil's lies and to help me accomplish God's will for my life," Matthew said. "I believe God has a specific purpose and plan for everybody's life, and I need more spiritual power to avoid all forms of sin. I was hoping you guys would be able to pray for me to receive the Holy Spirit's gifts so that I can be more obedient to God's will."

"We don't know how to pray that kind of prayer," Jamal said.

"Because we need more spiritual protection ourselves, maybe you would be so kind as to pray for us," Asad said.

"Maybe we should all pray together," Matthew said. "Would you like to pray in the lobby, or the main prayer hall toward the direction of Mecca?"

"Let's pray in the main hall," Jamal said.

As Jamal led the way into the main prayer hall through two tall arched doors, Asad turned toward two older gentlemen who were seated on the floor against the back wall and asked, "Would you like to join us in prayer?"

After everybody knelt in a row facing Mecca, Asad began by saying, "In the name of God, the Infinitely Good, the All-Merciful. Praise be to God, Lord of the worlds, the Compassionate and Merciful, Master of the Day of Judgment. Thee we worship and from Thee we seek help. Guide us upon the straight path, the path of those whom Thou hast blessed."

When Asad finished praying the first surah in the Quran, Matthew continued by saying, "O most Merciful and Compassionate, we come before you sinful, seeking more spiritual power in our lives. We know from the Quran that the demonic spirits under Iblis' control have the ability to tempt men into sin, and that sin will separate us from your fellowship.

"We also know from the Quran that you sent forth

the power of the Holy Spirit into Maryam's life, whose body was chaste, and she gave birth to the Messiah. We also know from the Quran that there was a reason why you sent the Messiah, and we accept the truth regarding the Messiah that has been revealed to humanity.

"Standing on the power of truth that you have revealed to humanity, we ask you to forgive all our sins and send forth the power of your Holy Spirit into our lives and hearts. We invite the Holy Spirit into our lives, hearts, minds, bodies and souls so that we can serve you in spirit and truth. We pray all these things through the powerful intercession of Isa Al-Masih."

After the men prayed together for the infilling of the Holy Spirit, they spent a long time discussing many different subjects in the Quran. When Matthew looked at his watch, he said, "I have to meet a friend, and I'm already running late. It was an honor praying with you. I wish I could stay longer because I could feel the power of the Holy Spirit moving among us. I have faith that our prayer will impart powerful changes in our lives."

"I hope you come back soon," Asad said. "I would like to introduce you to our Imam."

"That would be great," Matthew said as he headed toward the lobby. After looking around for Michelle, he noticed her standing beside an Islamic literature rack and said, "Sorry to keep you waiting. Are you ready to go?"

"I just need my shoes," Michelle said.

On the way back to the vehicle, Michelle asked, "Can I remove my headscarf now?"

"You had better leave it on until we get out of the parking lot," Matthew said. "The Imam lives in a house that's located on the property."

After driving about a mile away, Michelle said, "It felt like there was a heavy spirit of oppression at work on the women back there."

"I could feel some kind of religious spirit on the men's side," Matthew said.

"I think we should pray a cleansing prayer," Michelle said. "I want to take off my headscarf, but there's a fearful spirit of oppression that makes me feel like I need to keep it on, or worse, that I need your permission to take it off."

"Please remove your headscarf," Matthew said as he turned the corner and slowly coasted down a side street to park the 4Runner so they could pray a cleansing prayer together. "Heavenly Father, we thank you for the ministry opportunity at the mosque, but we know the demonic powers that operate behind false religions are very dangerous. We ask you to descend upon us with your cleansing power, strike down and destroy anything evil or demonic that has attached itself to us, and restore us to your Spirit-filled fellowship. In Jesus' name we pray."

"Thank you," Michelle said, "I needed a good cleansing prayer. There were only two older women in my section and they weren't very social."

"I was able to pray with some men, but it felt very awkward," Matthew said. "I referred to Jesus as Isa

Al-Masih, but I didn't want to pray in Allah's name, even though *allah* means 'God' in Arabic. I wish I could speak Arabic so that my prayers would sound more authentic."

"Maybe those men didn't know how to speak Arabic either," Michelle said.

"I'm still feeling inadequate," Matthew said. "Maybe because when I look at the life of Saint Paul, he was born a Jew, circumcised on the eighth day and was educated in strict accordance with the Jewish law at the feet of Gamaliel.[46] Paul had so much zeal for the Jewish religion that he persecuted the newly established churches.

"Then after he became a Christian, he could walk into any synagogue in the world and debate with the best and brightest Jewish rabbis, proving that Jesus was the Messiah. At the opposite extreme, here I am: I don't have any experience working with Muslims, I don't speak Arabic, I haven't read the Quran, and that was my first visit to a mosque."

"Didn't God say to Saint Paul, 'My grace is sufficient for you'?" Michelle asked.[47] "That's because God's power is made perfect in our weakness. God also chose the weak things of this world to shame the strong.[48] So if that was the first time you visited a mosque and you were able to pray with some men about the Messiah, then I can't wait to see what will happen once you develop your ministry strategy and acquire even more experience working with Muslims."

"Thank you for the encouragement," Matthew said. "It was a dark and hostile environment in there, and I feel like going back home to get some rest."

"I was hoping we could stop by the art gallery to see how Daniel is doing," Michelle said.

"I think we need to give Daniel greater leadership responsibilities," Matthew said. "If we are constantly micromanaging every move he makes, it will undermine his sense of confidence, and he will never develop into a powerful business leader. Besides, he wanted to meet with us at church tomorrow morning to discuss more Jewish success secrets."

* * *

The following morning when Matthew and Michelle arrived at the church, Daniel was working in the kitchen preparing lox bagels. He had already placed the smoked salmon, finely sliced cucumbers and red onions on a serving platter and was opening a jar of capers when Michelle walked into the kitchen to greet him. After offering to help him serve breakfast, Michelle asked, "How was the turnout at the art gallery?"

"There were more than a hundred Jclub members," Daniel said. "The owner was very happy, and I met this incredible Jewish girl named Rebecca."

"I thought you just got out of a relationship," Matthew said.

"Rebecca is not like that," Daniel said. "She's a very serious Christian who works for a Christian television station as an associate producer. We spent the entire evening together. It was such a blessing that you put me in charge of everything last night. With all those extra responsibilities, everybody was coming to me for help. I was able to introduce Rebecca to all our members, so she probably thought I was the most popular and successful guy in town."

"When do we get to meet her?" Michelle asked.

"She wants to get together for coffee early next week," Daniel said. "She heard about our healing seminar from an interview that she was conducting at the television station, and she wanted to check out our ministry. After discussing some outreach opportunities with her, I'm thinking she could help us with an advertising campaign or a promotional interview at her station."

"That would be a great blessing," Matthew said.

"When you were describing how you met Rebecca, I was thinking about how Isaac met his wife in the Book of Genesis," Michelle said. "God sent Abraham's servant on a long journey to his hometown to find a bride, and he chose Rebekah from all the other women, probably because she had a servant's heart and was willing to draw water for his camels."[49]

"Just think what would have happened if we never conducted the healing seminar," Matthew said. "You would have never written a letter to God asking his permission to date Aurora. If you never asked God's permission to date Aurora, you would probably still be hanging out with her.

"If you and Aurora were sitting at a table by yourselves, lusting over each other, Rebecca would have visited the art gallery last night, walked around for an hour and left disappointed. She would have wondered why God called her to visit a Jclub event in the first place."

"You're absolutely right," Daniel said. "That's exactly why it's so important that we remain completely faithful and obedient to Yeshua's will for our lives."

While Daniel was still speaking, Father O'Connor walked down the stairs and said, "Did the postal service drop off a package for me when the office was closed last week?"

"I haven't seen any deliveries," Matthew said.

"Would you like some lox bagels and tea?" Michelle asked. "They're delicious, and Daniel was just about to share some Jewish success secrets with us."

"I have several appointments today and have to get going," Father said, walking back up the stairs.

"If I were going to write a book on the Jewish success secrets, the first chapter would be about obedience to Yahweh's Word," Daniel said. "In the Book of Deuteronomy, Yahweh says, 'If you heed these ordinances, by diligently observing them,' then you 'shall be the most blessed of peoples.'[50] In this passage, Yahweh promises to bless the Jewish people if they diligently observe his ordinances.

"After studying this passage, I asked myself what ordinances is Yahweh talking about? What ordinances does Yahweh want us to diligently observe? The same promise is made in chapter twenty-eight when Yahweh said, 'If you will only obey the Lord your God, by diligently observing all his commandments that I am commanding you today,' then all these 'blessings shall come upon you and overtake you.'[51]

"It would seem that everybody wants to receive Yahweh's blessings, but very few people want to diligently observe his commandments. So to answer the question of what commandments Yahweh wants us to keep, I went back to the Book of Exodus when Yahweh called Moses to Mount Sinai and gave him the instructions to pass on to Israel.

"Yahweh said to Moses, 'These are the ordinances that you shall set before them.'[52] Because the ordinances begin in the Book of Exodus and continue through the Book of Deuteronomy, I'm assuming that Yahweh wants us to keep the entire Law of Moses.

"The next question I asked myself was: What would happen if the Jewish people failed to keep Yahweh's commandments and ordinances? Would Yahweh break his covenant and default on his promise? To answer that question, I turned to Saint Paul's letter to the Romans, where he said, 'What if some were unfaithful? Will their faithlessness nullify the faithfulness of God?'[53]

"Saint Paul answered that question by saying, 'By no means!'[54] He also made the same point in the Second Letter to Timothy when he said, 'If we are faithless, he remains faithful—for he cannot deny himself.'"[55]

"Are you saying there are so many Jewish billionaires and Nobel Prize winners because God remains faithful to his Word and continues to bless the Jewish people several thousand years after the birth of Christ?" Matthew asked.

"The promise extends a thousand generations, which would be approximately ninety thousand years," Daniel said. "In the Book of Deuteronomy, Yahweh says, 'Know therefore that the Lord your God is God, the faithful God who maintains covenant loyalty with those who love him and keep his commandments, to a thousand generations.'[56]

"After reading that passage, I read the genealogy in the Gospel of Matthew that says, 'All the generations from Abraham to David are fourteen generations; and from David to the deportation to Babylon, fourteen generations; and from the deportation to Babylon to the Messiah, fourteen generations.'"[57]

"Fourteen generations times three is forty-two generations," Michelle said.

"If the average person lives to be eighty years old, we could add another thirty generations from Yeshua's birth to the present, and still be well below the blessing threshold of a thousand generations," Daniel said.

"How do you propose that we apply this success secret to our lives?" Matthew asked.

"We could read the Torah with a fresh perspective to see how many of God's laws and ordinances we could apply to our lives," Michelle said.

"The Jewish people are the only religious group in the world who have tried to keep all of God's commandments described in the books of Moses and have failed," Daniel said. "Because Yahweh remains faithful in his promise to bless the Jewish people, it would help to explain why there are so many Jewish billionaires and Nobel Prize winners that come from such a small percentage of the world's population."

"Jesus didn't come to abolish the law and the prophets, but to fulfill them," Michelle said.[58]

"I find it deeply concerning that very few Christians have a desire to apply Yahweh's laws to their lives," Daniel said. "Take for example the Sabbath rest. The only mainstream religious denomination that I know of besides Messianic Jews who conduct church services on Saturday are the Seventh Day Adventists.

"Most Christians in America spend both Saturday and Sunday working, shopping and doing chores around the house. According to the Torah, the Sabbath should be a complete day of rest, a time of inactivity in God's presence, almost like a mini-vacation where we do nothing but rest and be refreshed in Yeshua's presence."[59]

"Thank you for sharing this with me," Michelle said. "I get so busy that I violate the Sabbath the entire weekend. I need to turn my phone off one day a week and spend more time in God's presence, reading God's Word."

"Another important directive from the Torah that

very few Christians want to follow is the Jewish kosher laws described in the Book of Leviticus," Daniel said.[60] "Everybody says that Yeshua declared all foods clean and that we can eat anything we want and never get sick, but that's not true, because the Book of Acts specifically forbids Christians from eating blood and the meat of strangled animals.[61]

"The reason Adonai placed pork on the list of unclean animals is because pigs are scavengers that will eat anything, including toxic waste. When a person feeds a pig industrial waste and other forms of garbage, all those harmful chemicals get trapped in the pig's flesh, and when we eat the pig, all those harmful chemicals will enter into our own bodies.

"The same is true with all scavengers, including shrimp and lobster. Adonai doesn't want us eating bottom-feeding fish, bugs, bats, snakes or scorpions. They are all listed as unclean foods in Yahweh's Word, and part of Yahweh's blessings for his beloved children is good health."[62]

"Thank you for sharing this with us," Michelle said. "I'm going to go through the Torah very carefully over the next several months to see how many of God's laws I can apply to my life."

"I will do the same," Matthew said.

"Another one of Adonai's laws that very few Christians in our modern-day churches want to follow comes from the Book of Leviticus," Daniel said. "The directive says that we should not 'tattoo any marks' on our bodies.[63] What part of that Scripture passage is so difficult to understand? Another directive says, 'A woman shall not wear a man's apparel, nor shall a man put on a woman's garment.'[64]

"Yeshua never gave Christians permission to get body piercings and tattoos or to dress up like transvestites for drag queen story time. It's all a form of worldliness that has crept into our churches, all because the majority of Christians don't think Yahweh's laws apply to them."

"I like it when Daniel gets all fired up and passionate over God's Word," Michelle said.

"I will keep working on the success secrets and share more with you next week," Daniel said.

"I also have some good news to share," Matthew said. "I have been working with a wealthy donor who is a retired cardiologist. His name is Doctor David Bennett, and he wants to support our short-term mission trips. He only wants to donate money to a nonprofit charity so that his donations would be one hundred percent tax deductible. I didn't want to tell you about this opportunity because it's extremely difficult to apply for and receive a 501(c)(3) tax-exempt status from the Internal Revenue Service."

"How long does it take to receive IRS approval?" Michelle asked.

"I submitted the paperwork last week," Matthew said. "The approval process can take several months. I applied under the name of African Missionaries. I didn't want to involve Jclub because, even though Jclub is a ministry, we also operate as a business for the purpose of making a living."

"I can hear the beat of the African drums already," Michelle said.

"While we are waiting for our tax-exempt status to be approved, Doctor Bennett has offered to pay for some camping supplies that we are going to need in the mission field," Matthew said. "He gave me his credit card and told me to purchase the best equipment possible."

"Who's going to run Jclub if everybody is away traveling?" Daniel asked.

"That's where you come in," Matthew said. "I'm thinking we need to give you greater leadership responsibilities in Jclub so that you can continue making a good impression on Rebecca."

"I would be happy to assume a greater leadership role," Daniel said.

11th CHAPTER

The following week when Daniel was distributing advertising flyers for the coffee shop meet and greet on the college campus, Matthew and Michelle made plans to visit several camping supply stores.

The most prestigious outdoor recreation store was located on Grand Avenue near the Lavender Hills shopping mall. When Matthew and Michelle walked through the front doors, they immediately noticed a thirty-foot-tall rock climbing structure in the center of the retail space.

"They offer free climbing lessons here, if you are interested," Matthew said.

"That sounds fun," Michelle said. "Check out that mountain bike display. Do they allow customers to ride around on bikes inside the store?"

"I'm not sure," Matthew said. "We need to buy a daypack that we can take on the airplane as a carry-on. We also need two larger backpacks that can be checked in with the airline as a fifty-pound piece of luggage. We

also need two lightweight tents with mosquito nets."

"Are we going to be sleeping outside?" Michelle asked.

"I'm not sure what to expect, but I want to be prepared," Matthew said. "We need to protect ourselves from mosquitoes so that we don't get malaria. If our hotel rooms don't have mosquito nets over the beds, we could set up our tents on top of the beds. That way, we could crawl inside our tents at night and be totally protected from those blood-sucking, disease-spreading flies."

After working with a salesperson to find the perfect-sized backpacks and warm-climate tents, Michelle said, "The prices seem a little high. Are you sure we have Doctor Bennett's permission to spend this much money?"

"He said that we should buy the best trekking supplies possible, of the highest quality, something that would last a long time," Matthew said.

"Is there anything else we need?" Michelle asked.

"We need two lightweight umbrellas, flashlights for when there's no electricity, a camping stove and a stainless steel pot to cook all our meals," Matthew said. "We should also buy some sunscreen and two backpacking towels."

"I have sunscreen at my house," Michelle said. "Why do we need a backpacking towel?"

"Because a cotton beach towel is way too big and bulky," Matthew said. "It would take up all the room in our backpacks. They make special towels that dry very fast, are lightweight and fold up into a shape smaller than a pair of socks."

"They also sell very expensive socks here as well," Michelle said.

"I think we need to travel with only two sets of clothes," Matthew said. "We need safari clothing that looks very professional. The people in Africa are always dressing up in their best attire. It's the strangest thing. It could be a hundred degrees outside in the dry, dusty African wilderness, and the pastors will be wearing dress shoes, dress pants, jackets and ties. The women usually wear brightly colored dresses with matching headscarves."

"Why only two sets of clothes?" Michelle asked.

"If I load the camping stove, food, water and stainless steel pot in my backpack, it would give you more room in your backpack for different variations of the same two outfits," Matthew said. "The plan would be to wash our clothes in the sink every night, and then as those clothes are drying, we would be wearing the second set of clothes the following day. We could also wash our clothes in a bucket, or in the river; then in the morning, we would have a fresh set of clothes to wear."

"That sounds economical," Michelle said.

"The difficult part of putting together the perfect outfits will be finding some comfortable walking shoes that function as hiking boots yet still look classy enough to blend in with the pastors who will be wearing dress shoes," Matthew said. "We also need lightweight safari clothing that dries fast and looks nice enough to wear with a jacket to church."

"I already have the perfect pair of classy walking shoes," Michelle said. "After we buy the backpacks and load all our essentials, it will give me a better idea of the weight and how much extra room I will have for additional clothing."

"Our backpacks could be so heavy that we wouldn't want to carry any more clothes," Matthew said. "Another option would be to buy some clothes in Africa. That way you could be dazzling in the latest African fashions."

"Is there anything else we need for the trip?" Michelle asked.

"We need a small bottle of food-grade hydrogen peroxide so that we can put a few drops in the highest quality bottled water that we can find," Matthew said. "It would also be nice to have a survival straw in case of an emergency, and a Bivy stick, but that might put us over our spending limit."

"What's a Bivy stick?" Michelle asked.

"It's an emergency satellite locator device that works anywhere in the world," Matthew said. "If our plane crashed in the Amazon rain forest or if we were stranded on a deserted island, we could press one button and the nearest emergency response team would know our exact location."

"If we were stranded on a deserted island, I would rather have a Bivy stick than another matching outfit," Michelle said. "How much does a Bivy stick cost?"

"I'm not sure," Matthew said. "Another option would be to skip the Bivy stick and trust in God's guidance by asking very specific questions about our destination. If we spend a lot of time practicing contemplative prayer, discerning the Lord's will for our lives, it may be possible to avoid dangerous situations in the first place."

"It sounds like we are in for an incredible adventure," Michelle said. "I'm so excited, and at the same time, so very thankful that we have time to prepare."

"Let's ask our salesperson to hold our shopping cart for a few hours," Matthew said. "That way we can visit several other camping supply stores, compare prices, examine the quality of the products, and make the best purchasing decisions possible based on prayer. We can also continue shopping several more days this week if you want."

"I would like that," Michelle said.

* * *

After spending several thousand dollars on the highest quality and most economically priced trekking equipment available, Matthew and Michelle met back at the church basement for the Wednesday morning business meeting. When they arrived, Daniel was preparing breakfast in the kitchen.

After serving blueberry muffins, cinnamon crunch bagels and freshly squeezed orange juice, Daniel said, "If the first Jewish success secret is based on God's promise to bless those who keep his commandments as described in the Torah, then the second success secret would be based on our willingness to impart those blessings to others."

"Can you give us an example?" Michelle asked.

"The Jewish people have been blessing their children for thousands of years," Daniel said. "The tradition started in the Book of Genesis when Israel wanted to bless his grandsons, Manasseh and Ephraim, by saying, 'Bring them to me, please, that I may bless them.'[65]

"After Israel imparted a blessing upon the boys, a controversy arose because Joseph wanted his father to place his right hand on the oldest boy, but his father refused. He explained his actions by saying the younger boy, Ephraim, would be greater than Manasseh, and that his offspring would become a multitude of nations.[66]

"From this situation, we not only see the importance of a blessing but also the spiritual power that flows from a blessing. In my family, we began the Sabbath on Friday evening. After lighting two candles, my parents would lay their hands on my brothers' and sisters' heads and invoke a spiritual blessing.

"For the male children, my father would say, 'May you be like Ephraim and Manasseh,' and then he would pronounce the benediction from the Book of Numbers."

"Do you have that verse number?" Michelle asked.

"It's located in the sixth chapter," Daniel said. "'The Lord bless you and keep you; the Lord make his face to shine upon you, and be gracious to you; the Lord lift up his countenance upon you, and give you peace.'[67]

"After blessing the male children, my mother would pronounce a blessing over my sisters by saying, 'May you be like Sarah, Rebekah, Rachel and Leah.' Then after invoking the benediction from the Book of Numbers, my parents would impart their own blessings over each child."

"Can you give us an example?" Michelle asked.

"My parents would always invoke a financial blessing of success over my life," Daniel said. "Although a parent's blessing may seem like nice words spoken to a child, they have a profound effect. When my father invoked a blessing over my life by saying, 'May you be like King David, a man after God's own heart,' it made me wonder about the life of King David.

"When my parents invoked a personal blessing of success over my life, it created a psychological drive that made me want to be successful. Because my parents wanted me to be successful, I had an early childhood obligation implanted deep within my heart that made me want to live up to those expectations.

"Because the vast majority of Jews are constantly blessing their children, I'm wondering how many of those deeply ingrained psychological drives have inspired, motivated or contributed to the success of so many Jewish millionaires and Nobel Prize winners, especially when the Jewish people make up such a small percentage of the world's population."

"When you were sharing your childhood blessings that your father imparted, it made me think about my high school friends, because their parents never had anything good to say about them," Michelle said. "The only words they would hear from their parents were, 'You're never going to amount to anything. You can't do anything right. You're such a failure.' Then some of the bullies in school would pick on my friends and echo those same curses over and over again.

"All those external messages became deeply ingrained into my friend's minds and hearts, and it didn't take long for them to develop into a self-fulfilling prophecy. Because these kids were constantly being devalued and cursed, it gave them an excuse to act out for attention. They were constantly getting in trouble and causing problems, and eventually, they started doing drugs. Many of them dropped out of school and ended up in jail."

"How do we apply this success secret to our lives?" Matthew asked.

"I want to be a blessing to everybody," Daniel said. "When we are constantly blessing other people, it will come back around to us through the principle of sowing and reaping.[68] If we are constantly sowing blessings into other people's lives, it will come back around to us as we reap greater blessings from our Heavenly Father. If I am constantly sowing curses into the lives of other people, how can I expect to receive blessings from my Heavenly Father?"

"I think we should start blessing all of our Jclub members," Michelle said.

"That makes a lot of sense," Matthew said. "We can start blessing one another in our words, deeds, actions and prayers. Once we get good at becoming a channel of God's blessings in our closest relationships, then we can expand those blessings to all our Jclub members."

"Thank you for sharing your success secrets with us," Michelle said as she stood up to hug Daniel. "You have been such a blessing to me ever since we met in Mr. McCormick's high school algebra class. May the Lord open the floodgates of heaven and bestow upon you every spiritual blessing, including an abundant outpouring of financial success and prosperity."

"That goes double for me," Matthew said. "May God bless the work of your hands, and may you be surrounded by successful and prosperous business leaders who will support, encourage and motivate you to accomplish your greatest potential. In addition, may the Lord, God Almighty abundantly bless all your friendships, relationships and business partnerships; in the powerful name of Jesus we pray."

"Speaking of relationships," Michelle said, "how was your time with Rebecca last night?"

"We have so much in common," Daniel said. "She grew up in an orthodox Jewish home, but after her oldest brother had an encounter with Yeshua, he converted his entire family to Christianity. After the family's conversion, Rebecca and her parents attended a Messianic Jewish congregation for several years. After that, Rebecca attended a Pentecostal church for several years because she wanted to operate with the gifts of the Holy Spirit. Now she's attending a Bible-based community church in Bridgeport."

"That sounds like a wonderfully diverse background," Michelle said.

"We get along so well together," Daniel said. "She even offered to help me deliver flyers on campus whenever her schedule permits. I haven't asked her about a television interview for Jclub yet, but I know she will help us."

"That would be a great blessing for us," Michelle said. "Maybe we could start with a radio campaign and then work our way up to television."

"I didn't want to bring this up today," Matthew said, "but I think we need to start fasting."

"Does this have something to do with Ramadan?" Michelle asked.

"Ramadan revolves around a lunar cycle," Matthew said. "I wanted to ask you to join me in a ten-day blender fast. Muslims fast thirty days during Ramadan, but from the articles that I have read, it doesn't sound very spiritual. Critics of the Muslim fast say their nights turn into day, and their days turn into night.

"Because Muslims cannot eat or drink water during daylight hours, they will stay up all night, eating, drinking and getting all their work accomplished. Then when morning comes, they will sleep all day only to start the process over again the following day."

"How does a blender fast work?" Daniel asked.

"I think we should set a time frame that works with everybody's schedule," Matthew said. "Keep in mind the fast will make us weak and tired and may interfere with our ability to sleep. It's usually a good idea to eat all the food out of your refrigerator before fasting in an attempt to remove all forms of temptations from your environment.

"The protocol for the fast is to consume around one thousand calories per day, by drinking only fruit or vegetable juice from a blender. In the morning, I like making a frozen fruit smoothie using apples, bananas, oranges, pineapple, pears or whatever other type of fruit is available. The fruit doesn't need to be frozen, but it makes a thicker smoothie, more like having ice cream for breakfast.

"For lunch, I usually blend an apple, two carrots, celery, half a cucumber, a slice of beet, red bell pepper and a small slice of ginger to make another smoothie. For dinner, I will cook a small piece of broccoli, some Italian squash, two tomatoes, a jalapeño pepper and a piece of garlic. Other times, I will add a carrot, red cabbage or a slice of onion.

"You don't want to cook the vegetables too long, because the heat will degrade the vitamins; so after cooking them for one or two minutes, I will pour the contents of the pot into the blender and make another smoothie in the evening."

"Everything sounds so healthy and delicious," Michelle said.

"The first few days are going to be difficult," Matthew said. "Our bodies will throw a fit. We will be weak and tired, but on the third day of the fast, our bodies will start burning fat for fuel. Our brains will release endorphins that will make us feel better, and by the third day we will be on a spiritual high."

"What kind of spiritual high?" Daniel asked.

"During the fast, we will feel a lot closer to God," Matthew said. "The words in our Bibles will come alive. You will be able to ask God questions and hear his softly-spoken answers more clearly. You may even develop a distaste for worldly activities that you would ordinarily engage in when you're not fasting.

"Watching television or listening to music may become so irritating that you will only want to curl up in a blanket and spend the evening communing with Jesus, the lover of your soul, in total silence.

"The main purpose of a fast is to draw closer to God, and because I have some important decisions to make, I want to convert all my hunger for food into a hunger for God. I want to be able to enter into God's presence, ask the Lord some very important questions and listen for the answers. I want to hear very clearly from God regarding the direction of my life and ministry efforts."

"I need to hear from Adonai regarding my relation-ship with Rebecca," Daniel said. "I made a promise to Yeshua that I would never date another woman without receiving his permission. I'm already several weeks into my relationship with Rebecca, and we are starting to make a lot of plans together, so it's time for me to get very serious in prayer to seek his approval."

"Count me in too," Michelle said. "My only concern is our omega-3 fatty acids."

"One option would be to take a spoonful of fish oil with your vegetable juice at night," Matthew said.

"You could also add some ground flax seed powder or flax seed oil into your fruit smoothie during the day, or take fish oil supplements with your multi-vitamins in the morning.

"The blender fast is the healthiest way to fast because of all the vitamins and minerals that we will be receiving. There are so many health benefits to fasting that I think everybody should conduct a little research on the Internet in an attempt to eliminate any fears or doubts you may be experiencing."

"I will research the health benefits of fasting for our next meeting," Michelle said.

"If we start cutting back on our normal diets this week, then next Wednesday we can start eating fresh fruit and vegetables as described in the Book of Daniel for a few days," Matthew said. "Then on Friday, we can start the blender fast. We will probably feel terrible over the weekend, but on Monday, we will be on a spiritual high the rest of the week."

"I was planning on meeting some friends at the bluegrass festival on Saturday," Michelle said. "Would you like to come with us?"

"I will let you know how I'm feeling Friday night," Matthew said. "If we start the blender fast on Wednesday, we should be feeling fine on Saturday, but keep in mind the fast will elevate us to a higher level of contemplative spirituality. There may be way too much noise, confusion and activity at the bluegrass festival, so you may want to create a contingency plan."

* * *

The following week, Matthew spent most of his time working with Doctor Bennett to set up short-term mission trips. Daniel began taking on a greater leadership role and recruiting more new members, while Michelle spent most of her time conducting women's Bible study groups and ministering to the younger members of Jclub.

Halfway through the fast, Matthew stopped by Michelle's house to see if she was available to spend the afternoon together. When Michelle opened the door, she hugged Matthew and asked, "How are you feeling?"

"I feel great," Matthew said as he took a seat on the front porch swing.

"You're right about being on a spiritual high," Michelle said. "I feel so much more contemplative and closer to God."

"My prayer time has been incredible as well," Matthew said. "I started writing healing letters to my ex-fiancée and my mother. After experiencing a profound breakthrough, I wanted to talk with you about dating. I was hoping we could spend the afternoon at the park."

"That sounds great," Michelle said. "Let me grab a water bottle and my jacket."

12th CHAPTER

Missionaries

Aspen Grove Park was located alongside the Grand Rapids River on the edge of town. The lake in the center of the park was surrounded by vast meadows of aspen groves and tall native grasses. The park was home to a thriving habitat of deer, rabbits, chipmunks, ducks and geese.

As Matthew and Michelle walked along the path that curved around the contours of the lake, Michelle said, "I have been researching the health benefits of fasting, and I was surprised to find increased brain function at the top of the list. Fasting also boosts a person's immune system and increases healing by decreasing the body's inflammation.

"Many people have been healed of high cholesterol and arthritic conditions by fasting. When we stop eating food all week, our bodies will start burning fat for fuel, which will in turn lead to weight loss. When given enough time, our bodies will start clearing out all the plaque and other debris that gets trapped inside

a person's arthritic joints. It also gives our digestive systems a break, has the ability to heal acid reflux and stomach ulcers, and motivates our bodies to replace old toxic cells with healthy new cells."

"I have been studying Scripture passages about fasting," Matthew said as he took a seat on a park bench. "Did you know that Moses spent forty days and nights on Mount Sinai in the presence of God without eating or drinking anything?[69] Then in the Book of Acts, all the Apostles fasted. Daniel and his companions would rather eat raw vegetables and water than defile themselves with food from the king's table; and of course, Jesus fasted forty days and nights in the wilderness."[70]

"Did Daniel tell you that Rebecca wanted to join us during the fast?" Michelle asked.

"I didn't know that," Matthew said.

"I think it's so sweet," Michelle said. "When Daniel told Rebecca about the ten-day blender fast, she not only wanted to support his efforts, but she wanted to experience a deeper and more intimate relationship with Jesus at the same time."

"It looks like we are going to receive approval from the Internal Revenue Service for African Missionaries," Matthew said. "Are you sure you're okay with trusting Daniel with more Jclub responsibilities?"

"I trust Daniel completely," Michelle said, "but I'm curious why you wanted to talk about dating."

"I wanted to define some terms with you regarding the differences between secular dating and Christian courtship," Matthew said. "It seems the word *dating* can mean almost anything to anybody. For example, one person might say, 'I dated a few times in college, but it was nothing serious.' Another person might say, 'I enjoy dating several people at the same time in an attempt to find my soul mate.' While another person might say, 'I'm involved in a very serious dating relationship.'"

"What do people say after going on a blind date?" Michelle asked.

"Secular dating usually implies going to bars to find the perfect person that you feel a connection with or find physically attractive," Matthew said. "In these relationships, both parties are usually on their best behaviors, trying to impress the other person for the purpose of pursuing sexual intimacy.

"Once a couple crosses sexual lines, they usually have a conversation making their dating relationship exclusive, meaning that they are not allowed to date other people or have sex outside of their exclusive relationship.

"If these types of relationships can grow in maturity without any major conflicts, the man will usually propose to his girlfriend on a romantic getaway, and the couple will get married. After spending the next nine months planning a wedding together, the couple will take vows to love each other for life. Unfortunately, half of these unions end in divorce, with the most common reason being irreconcilable differences."

"That's an interesting perspective," Michelle said. "How does Christian courtship work?"

"In Christian courtship, a couple is not allowed to have sex outside of a God-approved marriage, so the couple spends their time and energy being real and honest with each other," Matthew said. "They want to develop a deep, authentic and emotionally intimate relationship as they explore the possibilities of marriage.

"Once a couple completes a comprehensive and serious discernment process, which involves positive interactions with their extended family members, the next step is to seek God's permission before betrothal.

If a couple has God's permission to get married, then betrothal would be a lot more serious than an engagement.

"When a couple is engaged to be married, either party can become disengaged at any point in time and back out of the commitment. When a couple has God's permission to be betrothed and that couple gets married in the Catholic Church, the union becomes an indissoluble bond that cannot be broken."

"That sounds very serious," Michelle said.

"That's why I wanted to talk to you about the Christian courtship process," Matthew said. "If Christians are not allowed to have sex until marriage, then Christian couples shouldn't engage in physical intimacy until marriage. That's because a little physical intimacy will only lead to a greater desire for more physical intimacy, which will eventually give birth to sin.

"So if a Christian man wants to court a Christian woman and he's not ready to get married, how would that couple move their relationship forward without any kind of physical intimacy?"

"I'm not sure," Michelle said.

"The Christian courtship process seems to be missing a step," Matthew said. "What would be the next step for a Christian couple to move their relationship forward if it was somewhere between the courtship and betrothal process?"

"Maybe we could call the next step the spiritual alignment phase," Michelle said. "Let me think about it, and we can talk more in a few days."

* * *

The following day, Michelle arrived early at the church basement with a small bag of limes and started making tall glasses of lime water. When Matthew and Daniel arrived about ten minutes later, she handed them a glass and said, "It's only twenty-two calories."

"How have you been feeling?" Matthew asked.

"My body is experiencing some physical weakness, but I love the power that I'm experiencing in my spiritual life," Daniel said. "I can't believe the incredible closeness that I have been experiencing with the Holy Spirit as I meditate on Adonai's Word. I was able to ask Yeshua if I had his permission to date Rebecca, and I felt that I have his blessing, almost as if Rebecca and I were meant to be together."

"Congratulations," Michelle said. "I'm so happy for you. After you told me Rebecca wanted to fast with us, I started praying that she would have a good experience. I could feel so much love for her in my heart."

"Thank you for your prayers," Daniel said. "Were you able to receive any spiritual breakthroughs during your quiet times?"

"After Matthew told me he had been writing more healing letters, I started working on some of my underlying issues so that I could be more dependent on the Lord," Michelle said.

"During my quiet time, I was feeling called to work with the Muslims in Africa," Matthew said. "Were you able to hear anything from the Lord when you asked him about a short-term mission trip?"

"I'm not hearing anything," Michelle said.

"I also wanted to share a few tips on how to break the fast," Matthew said. "I'm planning to fast a few more days, but when you are ready to break your fast, it's important to restart your digestive system very slowly."

"How does that work?" Daniel asked.

"Do you remember how we slowly tapered off our regular diets and started eating fruit and vegetables for several days?" Matthew asked.

"I remember," Michelle said.

"When you break a fast, it's the exact opposite," Matthew said. "If you try eating a thirty-two-ounce porterhouse steak, it will make you sick, so you may want to start with some fresh fruit. A few hours later, try a little rice, or maybe some cooked vegetables. It's also important that you drink a lot of water as you slowly work your way back into your regular diet."

"I was thinking about breaking my fast with a cantaloupe," Michelle said.

"I also wanted to invite you to the Luxembourg Hotel for Sunday brunch," Matthew said.

"La-di-da," Michelle said. "What's the special occasion?"

"I think we all deserve a treat after going ten days on juice and water," Matthew said. "I also have some important announcements to make, and I think it would be wonderful if Rebecca could join us."

"Were you thinking about this weekend?" Daniel asked.

"I think this weekend is too soon," Matthew said. "We need to give our digestive systems more time to recover. I was hoping you could check with Rebecca's schedule and inquire about the last Sunday of the month."

* * *

Early in the morning, on the last Sunday of the month, Daniel picked up Rebecca at her apartment and arrived at the hotel a few minutes early.

The Luxembourg Hotel looked more like a country club than a hotel because the twelve-story, castle-shaped building was surrounded by a world-class golf course.

Instead of parking in the main lot, Daniel drove his BMW past a circular fountain that was surrounded by a lavender flower garden and then through a series of towering arches that were located near the main entrance, so that the valet could park his car in a private lot. Matthew and Michelle arrived a few minutes later and spent several minutes walking around the grounds, before meeting Daniel and Rebecca in the main lobby.

As the young couples were getting acquainted, a hostess approached them and said, "Your table is ready. If you will, please follow me."

The first room that the hostess led the missionaries through contained a five-foot-tall ice sculpture in the shape of a swan. "This is our main serving area," the hostess said as she continued her tour by passing by what seemed to be endless tables covered in white tablecloths, each containing an elegant display of entrées.

On a long table in the center of the room, there were artistically shaped rows of shrimp, lobster tails and crab legs. Other tables contained stainless steel containers with breakfast entrées. There were several omelet chefs working behind semi-circular serving stations, a waffle bar with every topping imaginable, and a vast display of tropical fruit.

The next room the hostess passed through contained bakery items, exotic desserts and a variety of drink options. In the third room, the couples were seated near a water fountain next to a bay window overlooking the golf course.

During the meal Daniel said, "I have some good news to share with everybody. When I was driving home last night, I passed by the strip club and the parking lot was completely empty. Because the building was dark, I turned around to go back and investigate. There was a sign on the door stating that the business had closed. I was so happy that I removed the sign from the door, threw it in the dumpster and started worshiping Yeshua for his mighty power."

"That's wonderful news," Michelle said. "I'm not sure if Rebecca has heard the full story, but we started praying over that property almost a year ago. Every day we were asking God to remove that business from our community, and month after month there have been fewer cars in the parking lot at night. I'm so happy that I would like to go back and pray over the parking lot one more time, thanking God for his miracle-working power."

"I also have some important announcements that I would like to share," Matthew said. "We finally received approval from the Internal Revenue Service. African Missionaries is now a fully functional 501(c)(3) non-profit charity that can accept all forms of donations for the purpose of spreading the Gospel message in the poorest countries of the world."

"Congratulations!" Michelle said. "I know how hard you have been working to get that set up."

"It gets even better," Matthew said. "Doctor David Bennett is ready to fund our short-term mission trips whenever we are ready to go on the next adventure."

"That's wonderful news!" Daniel said.

"He only has one condition," Matthew said. "He wants his donations used in a way that creates the maximum amount of heavenly treasure possible."

"Can you give us an example of how that works?" Daniel asked.

"He wants the maximum return on his money the same way a Wall Street banker would want the maximum return on his client's stock market portfolio," Matthew said.

"He sounds like a very wise man," Rebecca said.

"Think about that for a second," Matthew said. "When you invest your money in the stock market, you would have the choice of buying stocks, bonds, commodities or treasure notes. If you invested your money in a high-risk startup company that went bankrupt, you would not only lose any hopes of making interest on your investment, but you would probably lose your entire principal balance as well.

"The same would be true for investing in the kingdom of heaven. If we took Doctor Bennett's hard-earned money and gave it away to some poor people living in a slum, it may make those people feel better for a short amount of time; but what's going to happen to the doctor's interest that he wants to receive on his investment if all those people end up eternally separated from God?"

"I'm assuming the doctor would view that charitable contribution the same way a stock broker would view an investment in a company that went bankrupt," Daniel said.

"If we took Doctor Bennett's hard-earned money and gave it away to a Satanist, Buddhist monk or an atheist—just because they were poor—and all those people ended up in the lake of fire because they never accepted the Lord's sacrifice of the cross for the forgiveness of their sins, then I'm assuming the doctor wouldn't receive a very good rate of return on his investment.

"That's why I made a promise to spend all of our financial partner's donations in a way that would generate the greatest amount of heavenly treasure possible. In obedience to the Great Commission, the first priority of African Missionaries is to make sure everybody has entered into a life-saving relationship with our Lord and Savior, Jesus Christ.[71]

"Our second priority is to help the poorest of the poor by loving, caring and ministering to the orphans, widows and those living in extreme poverty, not only with life-saving resources, but also through the power of the Gospel message so that they can enter into a life-saving relationship with Jesus."[72]

"This is so exciting," Michelle said. "I can't wait to visit Africa."

"After spending a lot of time during the fast praying about the direction of my life, I'm feeling called to minister to the Muslims in Africa," Matthew said. "I want to deliver the Gospel message to every non-believer in the poorest countries in the world, and because I may not be around much longer, I would like to resign my position as the president of Jclub."

Because everybody at the table remained silent for what seemed to be a very long time, Matthew continued his announcement by saying, "I think we need to make Daniel the new president of Jclub, and I would like to invite Michelle to join me on an adventure of a lifetime."

After removing a small black box from his jacket pocket, Matthew said to Michelle, "I wanted to ask you to join me on the adventure of a lifetime—not only as a trusted ministry partner, a fellow evangelist or even as my best friend—but as my wife."

When Matthew opened the box that contained a two-carat diamond engagement ring, he proposed to Michelle by saying, "Will you marry me?"

To be continued in *Missionaries—Volume Two*
The Inner-City Homeless Adventure

Notes

Excerpts from the *Catechism of the Catholic Church* are quoted from the character's memory and are based on the English translation of the *Catechism of the Catholic Church* for use in the United States of America, © 1994, United States Catholic Conference, Inc.—Libreria Editrice Vaticana. English translation of the *Catechism of the Catholic Church*: Modifications from the Editio Typica copyright © 1997, United States Catholic Conference, Inc.—Libreria Editrice Vaticana. Used with permission. All rights reserved.

Excerpts from the English translation of the Quran are quoted from the character's memory and are based on Marmaduke Pickthall's *The Meaning of the Glorious Quran*, an Explanatory Translation (New York, NY: Alfred A. Knopf, 1930). Used with permission. All rights reserved.

Interior illustrations by NightCafe Studio Art Generator. All rights reserved.

1. Joshua 1:9 & Joshua 1:3.
2. 2 Corinthians 6:14–18.
3. 1 Corinthians 7:8.
4. Genesis 2:18.
5. 1 Corinthians 7:27–28.
6. 1 Corinthians 7:32–34.
7. Matthew 22:30.
8. 2 Corinthians 11:24–28.
9. 1 Samuel 10:6 & 1 Samuel 10:10.
10. Matthew 6:24 & Luke 16:13.
11. 2 Kings 2:20.
12. 2 Kings 2:21.
13. The creation story along with the fall of humanity is described in surahs 2:30–39, 7:19–27 & 20:115–123. The conflict between Cain and Abel is described in surah 5:27–32. Noah's ark and the

great flood is described in surahs 7:59–64, 10:71–73, 11:25–48, 23:23–28, 26:105–121, 54:9–16 & 71:1–28.

14. The destruction of Sodom and Gomorrah is described in surahs 7:80–84, 15:57–77, 26:160–174, 27:54–58, 29:28–35 & 37:133–138. Jonah and the whale is described in surahs 10:98 & 37:139–148. Joseph's life and how he forgave his brothers is described in surah 12:4–102.

15. The virgin birth of the Messiah is described in surahs 3:42–49, 19:16–35, 21:91 & 66:12.

16. The miracle of Jesus raising the dead is described in surah 3:49 & 5:110. The miracle of Jesus healing the man born blind is described in surah 3:49 & 5:110.

17. Surah 2:285.

18. Surah 4:136.

19. Romans 4:4.

20. Romans 6:23.

21. Surah 3:19.

22. Matthew 6:10.

23. Matthew 6:14–15.

24. Matthew 18:23–35.

25. 2 Corinthians 11:24–28.

26. Acts 19:11–12 & Acts 28:7–9.

27. John 8:12.

28. 1 Corinthians 9:24–27.

29. Psalm 103:12.

30. 2 Corinthians 6:14.

31. Ephesians 1:1.

32. *Catechism of the Catholic Church*: 823, Acts 9:13, 1 Corinthians 6:1 & 1 Corinthians 16:1.

33. *Catechism of the Catholic Church*: 2664.

34. Hebrews 12:1, Revelation 6:9–11, Revelation 7:13–14 & Revelation 8:3–4.

35. Jeremiah 44:2–27 & Jeremiah 7:16–18.

36. 1 Corinthians 6:13.

37. Matthew 5:27–29.

38. Hebrews 13:4.

39. 1 Corinthians 6:15–20.

40. Surah 23:97.

41. Surah 2:102.

42. Matthew 23:13–33 & John 8:42–44.

43. Surah 66:12.

44. Surah 21:91.

45. The Quran says that Jesus is the Messiah, a term used eleven times in surahs 3:45, 4:157, 4:171–172, 5:17, 5:72, 5:75 & 9:30–31.

46. Acts 22:3 & Philippians 3:5–6.

47. 2 Corinthians 12:9.

48. 1 Corinthians 1:26–29.

49. Genesis 24:1–67.

50. Deuteronomy 7:12 & Deuteronomy 7:14.

51. Deuteronomy 28:1–2.

52. Exodus 21:1.

53. Romans 3:3.

54. Romans 3:4.

55. 2 Timothy 2:13.

56. Deuteronomy 7:9.

57. Matthew 1:17.

58. Matthew 5:17.

59. Exodus 20:8–11 & Exodus 31:12–17.

60. Leviticus 11:1–47.

61. Acts 15:20.

62. Deuteronomy 7:12–15.

63. Leviticus 19:28.

64. Deuteronomy 22:5.

65. Genesis 48:9.

66. Genesis 48:17–20.

67. Numbers 6:24–26.

68. 2 Corinthians 9:6 & Galatians 6:7.

69. Exodus 34:28.

70. Acts 13:2, Acts 14:23, Daniel 1:8–16 & Matthew 4:2.

71. Matthew 28:18–20.

72. John 14:6.

Missionaries

The Inner-City Homeless Adventure

The adventures of Matthew Goodwin and Michelle Nobility continue as they transition away from their Christian-singles healing ministry and into a more challenging inner-city homeless environment. In their efforts to proclaim the Gospel message to drug addicts and alcoholics, they encounter an even more sinister presence of darkness.

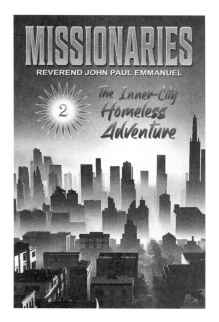

Available at your local bookstore or online.
www.ValentinePublishing.com

Missionaries
The Rural African Village Adventure

After being warned that their ministry destination was particularly dangerous, Matthew and Michelle exchange a tearful farewell with their friends and family before boarding a flight to Africa. With demonic forces lurking around every corner, the missionaries press through many trials and tribulations before obtaining the ultimate victory in Christ.

Available at your local bookstore or online.

www.ValentinePublishing.com

African Missionaries

Please consider supporting Matthew and Michelle's outreach ministry by making a tax-deductible donation to African Missionaries.

African Missionaries is a 501(c)(3) non-profit public charity that conducts mission trips to the poorest countries of the world for the purpose of spreading the Gospel message.

You can make an online donation by visiting www.ValentinePublishing.com or by sending a check to the following address:

African Missionaries
PO Box 27422
Denver, Colorado 80227

Please support our outreach ministry by distributing copies of *Missionaries, Volumes One, Two & Three* to your friends and family members.

To purchase a three-volume set, please use the following information:

Three-Volume Set	Ministry Price
One Set	$29
Two Sets	$59
Three Sets	$89

These prices include tax and free shipping within the United States. For shipments to other countries, please contact us. Thank you for your generous support.

Please mail your payment to:

Valentine Publishing House
Missionaries — Volumes One, Two & Three
PO Box 27422
Denver, Colorado 80227